BARRON'S PARENTING KEYS

KEYS TO DEVELOPING YOUR CHILD'S SELF-ESTEEM

Carl E. Pickhardt, Ph.D.

Cover photo by FPG International

DEDICATION

Thanks to my wife, Irene, for her editorial advice in the final stages of this manuscript, and to the Barbara Bauer Literary Agency for getting my writing to market.

Material in this book is drawn from counseling and from conducting workshops about helping to nurture children's self-esteem. All examples and quotes given, however, are fictitious—inventions created to illustrate a psychological point.

All inquiries should be addressed to:
Barron's Educational Series, Inc.
250 Wireless Boulevard
Hauppauge, New York 11788
http://www.barronseduc.com

Library of Congress Catalog Card No.: 99-56439

International Standard Book No.: 0-7641-0847-6

Library of Congress Cataloging–in–Publication Data

Pickhardt, Carl E., 1939–
Keys to developing your child's self-esteem / Carl E. Pickhardt.
p. cm. — (Barron's parenting keys)
Includes bibliographical references and index.
ISBN 0-7641-0847-6
1. Child psychology. 2. Self-esteem in children. 3. Child rearing. 4. Parent and child. I. Title. II. Series.
HQ772 .P49 2000
649′.7—dc21 99-56439
CIP

PRINTED IN THE UNITED STATES OF AMERICA
987654321

CONTENTS

Part Three—Nurturing Self-Esteem During Childhood

Part Four—School and Self-Esteem

Part Five—Nurturing Self-Esteem During Adolescence

Part Six—Destroyers of Self-Esteem

INTRODUCTION

S*elf-esteem is not real* in the sense that it can be visually examined, physically touched, or directly observed. Like *intelligence* or *conscience*, self-esteem is an *abstract* psychological concept made up to describe part of human nature. The existence of such an invisible entity only becomes concrete through personal actions and expressions considered to show evidence of its presence.

Thus, when a child solves a problem, this may be considered evidence of *intelligence.* When a child acts in accord with his or her beliefs about moral right, this may be considered evidence of *conscience.* And when a child demands to receive fair treatment, this may be considered evidence of *self-esteem.*

Proposed over a hundred years ago by American psychologist William James, self-esteem was first presented as a kind of formula: *self-esteem equals a relationship between accomplishment and aspiration.* This formula implied that people could feel better about themselves either by accomplishing more or by aspiring for less. (See Suggested Reading, Seligman, p. 30.)

This link between degree of accomplishment and level of aspiration is still a part of how psychology approaches self-esteem. For example: if personal achievement falls short of one's aspirations, lower self-esteem can result; but if personal achievement exceeds personal aspirations, higher self-esteem can result.

Today, however, the formula seems to have been adjusted to better fit the values of our contemporary culture: *self-esteem arises from the interaction between performance and personal worth.* Doing well for oneself can encourage feeling well about oneself, and feeling well about oneself can encourage doing well for oneself. Either way, with heightened performance or personal worth, self-esteem can be enhanced.

Where does self-esteem grow from, and when does it begin? According to the American Academy of Pediatrics, self-esteem is not inborn. It is something an infant begins to learn soon after birth through circumstantial experience and treatment from others and by interacting with the world. (See Suggested Reading, Schor, p. 125.)

The Popularity and Power of Self-Esteem

Self-esteem is one of those psychological concepts that have become so current in popular thought that it has crossed over into common use. Parents will often seek counseling help, for example, because they are concerned about their child's feelings of "low self-esteem." In the public schools, teacher and counselor training programs often emphasize strategies for enhancing the good feeling side of pupil self-esteem in the belief that *students who feel better about themselves become more motivated to do better for themselves.*

Perhaps the best clinical testimony to the enormous power of self-esteem is to see what happens when it falls perilously low, for example, when a child sinks into a major depression. Now a whole series of unhappy traits come to characterize the child's psychological world: pessimism, helplessness, hopelessness, anxiety, inadequacy, disinterest, discouragement, passivity, and apathy, among others.

This is why so much of recovery from depression depends on recovering self-esteem. As afflicted children begin to think better about themselves and act more effectively for themselves, positive self-esteem is restored. One doctor, who has worked with many depressed children, underscores the psychological power of strong self-esteem: "Over the years that I have practiced child psychiatry, I have come to believe this important idea: *Children with a healthy sense of self-esteem are the most resilient and best able to resist depression.*" (See Suggested Reading, Fassler, p. 184.)

The Approach to Self-Esteem in This Book

So, how can parents nurture their child's developing sense of self-esteem? Because there are so many ways, this book will only cover relatively few, selecting those *strategies* (what parents can *say* and *do*) that are located closest to hand, those rooted in the daily conduct of family life.

To this end, this book is organized as follows. Part One presents fundamental considerations about self-esteem—a working definition of the term, as well as the relation of self-esteem to responsibility, growth, learning, parental self-esteem, and similarity to parents. Part Two ties a child's self-esteem to four dimensions of family functioning—communication, courtesy, conflict, and correction. Part Three describes five ways parents can nourish a young child's esteem—by inviting help, placing money in perspective, encouraging creativity, fostering competence, and supporting competition.

Part Four presents three challenges of school life that if mastered can strengthen self-esteem—getting adequate grades, standing up to social cruelty, and (what is coming to be an important issue for many children) coping with ADD (Attention Deficit Disorder). Part Five explores some of the pitfalls for self-esteem built into the eight- to ten-year process of adolescence, common difficulties connected with developing gender role definitions, and how sexual orientation can affect self-esteem. Part Six is the most difficult section to read because it describes harsh, but unfortunately common, life experiences that can have devastating effects on a child's self-esteem—social oppression, depression, substance abuse and addiction, and abandonment and abuse.

Part Seven describes five life skills that children can be taught that can do much to strengthen their self-esteem—managing character, emotions, thinking, expectations, and stress.

At the end of the book are commonly asked questions about children and self-esteem that are not answered in the body of the text. A list of suggested readings is also included, as well as a glossary of unfamiliar terms.

A Final Word

If I didn't think self-esteem was important, I wouldn't have written a book about it. Within the matrix of concepts that explain psychological functioning, I believe self-esteem has a useful place. Important as it is, however, *strong self-esteem is not everything.*

For example, it is independent of morality. Strong self-esteem does not prevent wrongdoing. People who feel extremely positive about who and how they are can still become bullies, criminals, and even destructive zealots. *Evil can claim strong self-esteem as easily as can good.* Self-esteem is also independent of outcome. It does not assure accomplishment. People who feel confident about performing well are still capable of misunderstandings, miscalculations, and mistakes. *Strong self-esteem can lead a person into failure as well as to success.*

The concept of self-esteem is a very American one, particularly at home in our culture during the century that has followed its invention. Perhaps justified as part of our right to the pursuit of happiness and self-fulfillment, rooted in our emphasis on individualism, and nourished by our belief in self-improvement and material success, self-esteem is a notion that seems here to stay. In addition, it has a certain common sense appeal and validity, if not a scientifically verifiable one. Given a choice, most people would rather have high self-esteem than low because they link it to personal well-being and effectiveness.

As parents reflect on the esteem needs of their child, I hope they will also reflect upon their own, because *everyone's self-esteem in a family matters.* From my vantage point as a psychologist, it seems that people are more prone to act badly toward members of their family when they are feeling bad about themselves. The worse they feel, the worse they often treat others, the worse they get treated in return, the worse they end up feeling about themselves, the worse they treat others, and round and round the cycle of unhappiness goes. *In low-esteem families, relationships can become mutually destructive.*

In high-esteem families, however, the reverse seems more likely to occur. The better that family members feel about themselves, the better they treat each other, the better they get treated in return, the better off everyone tends to become. *They bring out the best in each other, not the worst.*

Positive self-esteem is not some kind of popular fad or new-age frill, it is an old-fashioned necessity. Upon its existence, the happy and healthy functioning of individuals and families partly depend.

IN SUPPORT OF SELF-ESTEEM

If people like me or they do not;

If I win or if I lose;

If I have lots of money or not very much;

If I am treated well or badly;

If I encounter fortune or adversity;

If I succeed or if I fail;

If I find love or I do not;

If I appear attractive or am rather plain;

If I am smart as others or not as smart;

If I feel well or I feel sick;

If I perform to my credit or to my blame;

Either way,

I will claim the self-respect that I deserve;

I will value who and how I am;

I will keep faith with the good that resides in me;

I will be grateful for all the human nature that is mine;

I will try to do what I believe is best and right;

I will forgive myself when I have not;

And I will work to improve myself the best I can.

Carl E. Pickhardt, Ph.D.

1

WHAT IS SELF-ESTEEM?

TWO CONCEPTS IN ONE

"Self-esteem" is two words compounded into one. Separate them, and the meaning of the larger term comes clear.

"Self" is a *descriptive* concept: By what specific *characteristics* do I identify who I am? "Esteem" is an *evaluative* concept: By what *criteria* do I judge the worth of who I am? *Self-esteem has to do with how a person describes and evaluates his or her definition of self.*

Variability

Over the course of anyone's life, self-esteem will fluctuate and vary. A person's esteem for self can rise or fall depending on wellness or illness, success or failure, gain or loss, freshness or fatigue, fortune or adversity, or a host of other changing circumstances and conditions that are a normal part of human experience. It is helpful for parents to keep this variability in mind. When they treat self-esteem like a constant that, once positively set, is never going to alter, parents can become easily mystified by their growing child's normal periods of self-discontent. In early adolescence and mid-adolescence, for example (see Key 19), intense and unpredictable mood swings can often cause the teenager to impulsively alter self-definition (appearance) and self-evaluation (approval) in ways that can dramatically raise or lower self-esteem. Parents must treat this ever-changing part of their child not as a problem to be stopped, but as a reality to be accepted. They must also help the child learn to take responsibility for defining and evaluating himself or herself (see Key 2) in order to recover or maintain strong self-esteem through the inevitable changes and challenges of growing up.

The Concept of Self ("How I Identify Myself")

The concept of "self" means little until the abstract term becomes connected to a specific dimension of a person's life with which he or she consciously identifies. So, in asking a child, "Tell me about your*self*," the little boy or girl may start describing interests ("I like sports"), status ("I am in the second grade"), relationships ("I live with my parents and a younger brother"), possessions ("I have a cat named Rufus"), knowledge ("I can tell you a lot about basketball"), or history ("One time we went to Mexico"). Each descriptor adds yet another dimension to the concept of self the child claims. (Needing to fill out their sense of self-definition, many adopted children feel the need to search out biological parents: "I know I'm part of the family I came up in, but I'm also part of the parents who gave me birth. And I need to claim that history to feel complete.")

"Self" is like a mansion with many rooms, in each of which the young person lives: "I am what I enjoy doing; I am who I know; I am how I feel; I am what I remember; I am my past; I am what I have; I am what I think about; I am where I belong;" and the list goes on and on.

Understanding this healthy diversity, parents should become concerned when it seems to shrink, when their growing child chooses to live in fewer and fewer "rooms." In a worst case situation, a child may only live in one room, which, when it becomes empty, can leave the child with a lack of esteem that feels overwhelming. "You know how social I am. Now that we've moved and I'm in a new school, I don't have any friends. I'm *nothing* without my friends!"

At this point, parents need to help the child fill up the missing room and develop furnished rooms to house additional self-definition. They can do this by hosting some social events to help their daughter make new friends. They can also encourage her into solitary activities in which she can learn to keep herself rewarding company. "We will help you reach out to friends, but we also want you to develop good-feeling ways to enjoy spending time with yourself." *Low self-esteem can result from a restricted or diminished definition of self.*

The Concept of Esteem ("How I Evaluate Myself")

The concept of esteem is an evaluative one that ultimately depends on how a child chooses to judge himself or herself. These judgments can be positive or negative, boosting or reducing self-esteem. Most commonly, they are based on:

- The *degree of attainment* of personal standards and goals, like in some area of achievement ("I didn't score a single point in the game today" or "I scored more points than I usually do")
- *Having one's performance graded* low or high by an external authority ("The coach took me out after the first period" or "The coach kept me in the whole game")
- *Making comparisons* between oneself and others, like how little or how much one has in contrast to how much others have ("The other kids all have more ability than me" or "I was able to keep up with the other kids")
- Receiving *external approval or disapproval* from others whose opinions are valued highly like peers ("Being booed for missing easy shots really hurt" or "Being cheered for

making the winning point felt really good")
- Entering some competition and *losing or winning* ("I feel like a loser when our team keeps losing" or "I felt we played well even though we lost")

Parents should assess if they have a highly judgmental child. If so, the harder on himself or herself the child may be, the more unbalanced that evaluation can become when something goes wrong, the more to heart any criticism can be taken. Therefore, a parent needs to be sensitive to children who (often similar to the parent) expect a lot from themselves, fault themselves easily, and forgive themselves grudgingly.

One way to counter this tendency to self-depreciation is to request a measure of *self-appreciation* to be included with each evaluation. Rather than disagree with the child's self-critical bent (which many such children will argue to defend), parents can encourage the boy or girl to include in his or her self-evaluation two other, equally important, components: *the willingness to take compliments* that are honestly given, and *the willingness to take credit* for what he or she is also doing well. "We respect your right to criticize yourself for how you performed, but we want you to evaluate the whole picture, not just part. Some of your play was good, and even though your shots were not falling, you hung in there and kept trying to do your best. The hardest time to keep going is when things don't seem to be going right. Good for you!"

Low self-esteem can result from an unduly critical evaluation of self. Parents can help the child recover from this kind of lost esteem by insisting on a balanced self-evaluation that not only admits failings, but acknowledges strengths as well.

2

RESPONSIBILITY

WHO IS IN CHARGE OF A CHILD'S SELF-ESTEEM?

Parents need to separate *influence on* from *control over* their children's self-esteem. Parents have a lot of *influence* because their love, treatment, approval, and example matter, and because they set terms on which the child lives at home. *Control*, however, ultimately rests with the boy's or girl's decisions about what and what not to do and how to feel.

This separation of responsibility is worth insisting on because when it is not in place, the child can make a statement reflecting this confusion: "You're making me feel bad about myself!" No. The parents can certainly behave in ways the child doesn't like, but *defining* and *evaluating* self (the twin components of self-esteem) are ultimately up to the child.

Parents can stress the importance of making this separation by recommending two rules of conduct.

1. "Don't let how other people identify you limit how you define yourself."

2. "Don't let how other people evaluate you determine how you judge the worth of yourself."

Separating Treatment from Self-Esteem

To take a worst case example, consider two children, X and Y, growing up with the same verbally abusive parents who nightly take out personal frustrations by tearing down the kids and blaming them for all their stress and strife. Counseling with X, the child talks about how bad he feels about himself in consequence of the harsh words he has received. "There must be something wrong with me for my parents to treat me so bad. After all, parents are supposed to love you, so I know it must be my fault." In this case, X gives himself a negative self-evaluation for his parents' destructive acts.

Counseling with Y, however, the child also talks about how bad the treatment feels; yet she does not feel bad about herself. *What makes the difference if the treatment is the same?* "I don't like it, but at least I know something is wrong with them and not with me. Parents aren't supposed to treat children this way." In this case, she spares herself a negative evaluation by assigning responsibility to the parents for their own destructive acts. Under the same extreme duress, the self-esteem of two children comes out very differently—X sacrificing esteem by blaming self, Y preserving esteem by placing responsibility where it belongs.

The Power of Behavior and Beliefs

Children's self-esteem is primarily up to them, and they need to be taught that power of choice. Through *behaviors* they take on, they *define themselves.* These actions can be *self-enhancing.* Continuing to try in the face of frustration, for example, tends to strengthen esteem. Other actions can be *self-defeating.* Giving up because the task is not proving easy, for example, tends to weaken esteem. In this situation, parents can use their influence to pressure or instruct. They can insist on or encourage continuation of effort in order for the child to learn to persevere when doing something hard. In consequence, the child can feel good about himself or herself for having seen a difficult project through. "Wow! I did it! I didn't think I could!"

Through *beliefs* they hold about themselves, children *evaluate themselves*. These judgments can be *self-enhancing*. Complimenting oneself for doing something successfully, for example, tends to strengthen self-esteem. Or, these judgments can be *self-defeating*. Labeling oneself "stupid" for making a mistake tends to lower self-esteem. In this situation, parents can influence the child's evaluation with their own: "We believe that making mistakes are just a normal part of how people learn." Adopting that evaluation, the child feels better about herself. "Now I know what not to do, and I didn't know that before."

So who is responsible for what?

- Managing his or her self-esteem is *the child's personal responsibility.*
- Teaching the child to manage his or her self-esteem is *the parent's instructional responsibility.*

Self-Enhancing and Self-Defeating Behaviors and Beliefs

Self-esteem is a function of how a child learns to treat himself or herself in enhancing and defeating ways. A parent must hold children accountable for their behaviors and beliefs that affect their own self-worth. To this end, a parent can identify what treatment is positive and what is negative, and explain to the child the reinforcing connection between beliefs and behaviors. All of this instruction is to educate the child to take more control over his or her self-esteem. Teaching about common self-enhancing and self-defeating behaviors and beliefs is how this instruction is done.

Examples of *self-enhancing behaviors* that parents could support might be: taking responsibility for one's own mistakes, accepting compliments, fixing something broken, completing what one starts, and keeping promises to self and others.

Examples of *self-enhancing beliefs* that parents could support might be: "I have a lot to offer," "I am helpful," "I have a good sense of humor," "People enjoy meeting me," "It's fun trying something new."

Examples of *self-defeating behaviors* that parents could identify might be: refusing to speak up in a group, having to control play with other children, not trying activities one might not be good at, lying to escape responsibility, and cheating to win.

Examples of *self-defeating beliefs* that parents could identify might be: "I don't have anything worth saying," "Nothing ever works out for me," "I can't do anything right," "If something goes wrong it's probably my fault," "If people really got to know me, they wouldn't like me."

The Connection Between Behaviors and Beliefs

The connection between these behaviors and these beliefs are important for the child to understand. Parents can explain that either one can have strong bearing on the other.

To a degree, *behavior is the outcome of belief.* For example, if a child thinks he or she is just as smart as other students, that child is more likely to try to do as well as most of the others in school. If, however, a child considers himself or herself inferior and stupid, that child is less likely to try to do as well as most other students. Why? Because *beliefs can operate like self-fulfilling prophecies* when they set expectations that the child strives to meet.

To a degree, *belief is the outcome of behavior.* For example, if a child is able to shinny up a tall tree the first time out without incident, that child might believe himself or herself to be a naturally good climber. If, however, the child takes a bad fall from part way up, that child might assume tree climbing was not something he or she was good at.

Why? *Because behaviors demonstrate what is true* by providing evidence that convinces people what to think.

By keeping to behaviors that cause the child to feel good about himself or herself, the boy or girl is more likely to engender beliefs in his or her self-worth. By believing in one's own self-worth, the boy or girl is more likely to behave in ways that generate good feelings about self.

So, what are the three instructional responsibilities parents have for their child's self-esteem?

1. *Look* for the self-enhancing and self-defeating behaviors, and let your child know what they are.
2. *Listen* for the self-enhancing and self-defeating beliefs, and let your child know what they are.
3. *Label* the connections between behaviors and beliefs, and let your child know what they are.

3

GROWTH

THE ONGOING CHALLENGE FOR SELF-ESTEEM

Growth can be hazardous to a child's self-esteem because of *painful losses* that must be sustained and because the *sequence of growth* itself can cause parents to respond in impatient and insensitive ways.

Losses from Growth

Why should there be any loss at all? Because *growing up means giving up*. In order to take on new ways of living within oneself, with others, and with the world, some old ways must be let go. Continual loss is the price a child must pay for continuing to grow. Just as the infant gives up the breast for the bottle, and the toddler gives up the bottle for the cup, so every step toward more independence is a step away from some dependence enjoyed before.

Of course, there are rewards to growth—more competence and responsibility, increased social standing, and approval in parental eyes. Relinquished comforts, however, are still missed, with the growing child associating them with a simpler time of life. For growth not to cost self-esteem, it helps if parents treat the child's inevitable losses with understanding, as the hard part of growing up. "Just because we take less care of you as you grow older, that doesn't mean we care about you any less. We love you as much as ever, and we respect you even more."

Parental criticism is usually the enemy of a child's self-esteem. So, in the case of losses engendered by growth, parents should not criticize their child for saying that they miss old indulgences ("I wish I hadn't grown too big for you to carry!"). Nor should parents get angry when their child occasionally regresses to reclaim old consolations that have been given up for growing up ("Read me to sleep just like you did when I was younger and got to feeling sick").

Best to remember that growing up is at best a clumsy dance, two steps forward and one step back, an alternating mix of progress and regress. *Parents who become impatient with this inconsistency, or who choose to punish the child for falling back, only add risk from their disapproval to an inherently risky process. In consequence, they can discourage advancement and endanger the child's self-esteem.*

It takes two acts of courage to grow, and enduring loss is only the first. The second is facing the insensitivity of parents who often do not understand the sequence of growth that is going on.

The Sequence of Growth

A growth stage begins when the child casts off old limitations to create new freedom for development to occur. Trying to keep pace with this emergent process can be confusing for parents. Playing catch-up is the best they can often do.

Whether it's the transition out of childhood into early adolescence (around ages nine to thirteen, see Key 19), or from the "wonderful one's" to the "terrible two's," parenting can never stay the same because the child is constantly changing. Just when parents feel they have their parenting "together" and their child figured out, he or she becomes different to live with and they wonder what is going on and how they should respond.

How they should respond is an important question, because their answer can directly enhance or injure their child's self-esteem at a vulnerable time when self-definition and self-evaluation are changing. It can be helpful at this juncture for parents to understand the general nature of whatever growth sequence their child is passing through.

GROWTH SEQUENCE

1: Disintegration of old definition	*2: Exploration* of the untried	*3: Consolidation* of new definition
	Motivation	
Dissatisfaction: Come apart by contesting old limits and breaking boundaries	*Curiosity:* Use freedom to experiment with new experience	*Control:* Come together to create new identity
	The child feels	
Restless: *"I don't like how I am or how I'm treated."*	*Excited:* *"I'm going to try on some new ways of acting."*	*Content:* *"I like the different way I have become."*
	The child seems	
Oppositional to parent	*Unpredictable* to parent	*Consistent* to parent
	The parent feels	
Angry at the resistance	*Anxious* from the unknown	*Relieved* by the stability

Separating Process of Growth from Personal Choice

Parents need to anticipate growth sequences as a normal part of their child's growing up and not take these changes personally or become overly severe in response. If they do, anger at opposition (from disintegration) can cause them to criticize and say hurtful things, and fear of the unpredictable (from exploration) can cause them to overreact to get control and do hurtful things. Parents need to accept the sequences of growth: how disintegration begets exploration, exploration begets consolidation, and sooner or later consolidation begets disintegration once again. Growth is *not* something children do to offend parents; it is something they do to develop themselves.

They should not blame the child for the process of growth, but they must hold the child accountable for the personal choices he or she makes as the process unfolds. Thus, they accept the two-year-old's frustration when freedom is denied (opposition as part of disintegration), but they let the child know that a tantrum will not reverse a parental "No." Thus, they accept the little child's urge to investigate by tasting what can be touched (experimentation as part of exploration), but they let the child know that street refuse is not to be placed in the mouth.

They don't treat growth as a punishable offense, but they do treat his or her decision making as their child's responsibility. And when their child's behavior evens out and he or she becomes placid to live with for awhile, they do not expect contentment from consolidation to last forever. They stand ready for the next burst of developmental change.

Where growth is concerned, children have a lot at stake because they are placing their self-definition and self-evaluation (the twin components of self-esteem) at risk of revision, with no guarantee of what the outcome will be. Growth takes courage—to enter the unknown and to brave parental impatience or disapproval. This is why children need parental acceptance for what instinct is compelling them to do, not censure for undergoing change over which they have no control.

4

EDUCATION

THE RISKS OF LEARNING

The relationship between self-esteem and learning is a tricky one. Although learning can enhance self-esteem by increasing skills and understanding, it can also require self-esteem to learn. Parents tend to appreciate the first part of this statement, but often do not respect the second. Why should it take self-esteem to learn? Because *the process of learning itself is a psychologically risky one*, and the willingness to take those risks partially depends on the child's sense of self-confidence and worth.

The Risks of Learning

Perhaps *instructional amnesia*—parents forgetting how, as children themselves, learning even the simplest tasks could be daunting and difficult to do—is part of the problem. In consequence, parents become impatient when their child can't quickly grasp some basic concept like safety when crossing a street. "Why can't you do it right the first time? It doesn't take a genius to understand! It's pretty simple. You're just supposed to go to the corner, stop, and look both ways. If there are no cars coming from either direction, then it's safe to cross to the other side. What will it take for you to learn?" The answer is: practice through repetition because *most children are not one-trial learners* when it comes to what their parents want them to know or know how to do. Parental patience, supervision, and encouragement are usually required. Get irritated and the child may refuse to learn because the process itself has come to feel *unsafe*. Unsafe how?

Consider a sixteen-year-old, who has never driven before, with a nervous parent for an instructor. Together in the car, with the child behind the wheel, the parent's safety is now dependent on the child's inexperience. Now consider *five risks to self-esteem* the child must brave to learn how to drive.

1. He or she must be willing *to declare ignorance.* "I don't even know how to shift gears."
2. He or she must be willing *to make mistakes.* "I didn't remember to take the emergency brake off before I accelerated."
3. He or she must be willing *to feel stupid.* "I meant to pull the turn signal, but I did the windshield wipers instead."
4. He or she must be willing *to look foolish.* "I stall at the intersection, and now all the drivers behind are honking at me."
5. He or she must be willing *to get evaluated.* "And now you're complaining that after the fourth try I'm still parked too far from the curb!"

Because learning develops competence, it supports self-esteem. At the same time, however, because learning always puts self-esteem at risk, parents need to be mindful of their responses as the child goes through this trial and error process of acquiring new skills and understandings.

Going back to the example of the parent as a nervous passenger, contrast two extreme sets of responses this parent could make to the five risks their novice driver is taking. Note *encouraging* responses on the left and *discouraging* responses on the right.

ENCOURAGING RESPONSE	LEARNING RISK	DISCOURAGING RESPONSE
"Not knowing is where all learning begins."	*Declaring ignorance*	"Not knowing better at your age is dumb."
"We all learn from the errors of our ways."	*Making mistakes*	"You just keep messing up."
"It's hard not to know."	*Feeling stupid*	"You'll never learn!"
"You're brave to keep trying."	*Looking foolish*	"What will other people think?"
"You've learned more than you knew before."	*Getting evaluated*	"You did it wrong again!"

If parents want to *discourage* their child from taking the risks of learning, electing to avoid new challenges to avoid getting hurt, they can do so by making responses that injure his or her self-esteem. They can make learning *unsafe* by:

- Putting down ignorance
- Being impatient with mistakes
- Criticizing for stupidity
- Embarrassing feelings of foolishness
- Giving punitive evaluations

In the process of doing all these things, they reinforce the child's reluctance to take some risks of learning that growth requires. If, however, parents see learning for what it is—an act of bravery—they will make *encouraging* responses instead. They will:

- Appreciate the willingness to admit not knowing
- Be patient with inevitable mistakes
- Sympathize with sometimes feeling stupid
- Compliment the courage to try and fail in public
- Give positive evaluations for learning more than was known before

Home Safety Measures

Finally, parents can make support of everyone's learning a family value. They can model patience in their own learning, not acting frustrated, discouraged, or upset with themselves when learning something new does not come easily. And they can make sure that no one gets puts down when they have a hard time mastering a new skill or understanding. Thus, older children are taught not to make fun of younger children in their struggles to learn.

5

PARENTAL SELF-ESTEEM

HOW THE MODEL MATTERS

There is a maxim in parenting that states: "You cannot give to your children that which you do not possess yourself." According to this principle, a parent who habitually lies cannot any more transmit honesty to a child than a chronically explosive parent can transmit staying calm in a crisis. What parents teach is based less on what they say than by their personal conduct. To the child: *how they act is what they instruct.*

So, when a parent gives that double message—"Do like we say, not as we do"—the model shown usually proves more powerful than the directive given. Told, by parents who want to spare a son or daughter their lifestyle stress, not to overcommit, run constantly behind, have to perform under pressure, and feel exhausted much of the time, the child still overdoes to his or her emotional cost. Why? To some degree a child learns how to act by imitating parental behavior.

Thus, when parents correct the child using the same behaviors they want the child to quit (yelling to stop the boy or girl from yelling, for example), they only end up encouraging the misconduct they were wanting to extinguish. Once again, the model shown proves more powerful than the instruction given. *For good and ill, leading by example is how parents influence their child the most.*

Modeling and Self-Esteem

Some modeling is intentionally given. Parents can reward the child with approval when he or she has learned to follow a rule or do a task their way: "Good for you, you did it just like us!" And the little child feels proud for acting as they do. Much of the modeling that parents give, however, is unconsciously provided and received. By parents acting spontaneously, children incorporate these examples automatically, becoming imprinted unawares. The little boy or girl acquires much self-definition as part of the family culture into which he or she is born, taking these learnings as much for granted as do the parents themselves—their habitual behaviors, general attitudes, unspoken assumptions, manners of speech, matters of taste, and the like. Most of this modeling escapes parental notice at the time, and that includes behaviors and beliefs that can directly affect self-esteem for good or ill.

This common oversight, however, can be corrected. If they wish, parents can assess their own *self-enhancing* and *self-defeating* beliefs and behaviors across several domains of their lives. They can inventory the possible influence of their modeling on the self-esteem of their child by answering three questions.

1. *On what self-enhancing and self-defeating terms do they live within themselves?* For example: are they self-accepting and appreciative or self-rejecting and critical; do they take care of themselves or do they neglect care for themselves; do they feel empowered by a sense of responsibility or do they feel whatever happens to them is up to someone else?

2. *On what self-enhancing or self-defeating terms do they live with other people?* For example: do they tend to treat those they know with trust and honesty

or with distrust and deception; do they tend to speak up and express themselves or shut up and remain in concealment; do they tend to reach out and engage with people or do they tend to withdraw and isolate?

3. *On what self-enhancing or self-defeating terms do they interact with the larger world?* For example: do they believe that trying hard is worth the investment or that effort is futile and a waste of time; do they believe in being active on their own behalf or in passively accepting whatever happens; do they feel hopeful about a future with opportunity or feel hopeless about a future with nothing but disappointment to offer?

Neither set of alternatives is right or wrong. Self-esteem is more likely to be higher if the positives are chosen, however, and this model is more likely to encourage growth of positive self-esteem in their child.

The Second Model Parents Give

There is an escape clause in the maxim of modeling with which this Key began. Parents can actually transmit to their child positive characteristics they do not possess that will enhance his or her self-esteem. At first, this sounds contradictory. Is the maxim wrong? No. The maxim is correct, but only as far as it goes because there is more to modeling than simple imitation.

There is also the conscious refusal to imitate. *Modeling is partly based on what parents have to give, but also partly on what children choose to take.* This means that each parent has *two* models to give their child, not just one:

- How to be
- How *not* to be

Simply put, children can make a decision *not* to be like their parent in ways they find painful, distasteful, unproductive, *or even defeating of self-esteem.* "When I feel bad about myself, I'm not going to get drunk like my mom, because I've seen how that just makes everything worse!"

In this case, the mother didn't mean to provide a negative example to give her child a positive model to follow, but that is what happened. *The child received the gift of the counter-model—of how not to be.*

Changing the Model

Once the parental model is set, does that mean it is forever fixed? For example, consider a man who grew up in a family ruled by perfectionist parents for whom no amount of achievement was ever deemed good enough. Not any harder on him than they were on themselves, they only taught him what they themselves were taught: to never feel self-satisfied, to always strive for ideals that could never quite be reached, to never feel good enough. So the man, now a parent himself, is plagued by feelings of personal inadequacy, his self-esteem constantly under internal attack: "I could have tried harder; I might have done better; I failed to do my best; I've fallen short of my potential; I'm never going to measure up to the man I should be."

This is the model for self-esteem that he sets and, through constant criticism, conveys to children of his own. Can he change this model if he chooses? Or is he doomed to pass on the sense of inadequacy he learned to another generation?

The answer to this last question is most assuredly "No." As mentioned earlier, self-esteem is based on how a person *chooses* to define himself and *chooses* to evaluate that definition. In the example above, self-esteem is the outcome of how the man learned to treat himself in self-defeating ways.

He can change the terms on which he lives within himself, however, by lowering the standards he wants to live up to from inhumanely ideal to realistically humane. And with practice, he can come to terms with the notion that being imperfectly human is good enough for most people and so is good enough for him.

Recovery from self-defeating behavior happens all the time, and when it happens in the life of a parent, the change can be extremely liberating for the child. The modeling power of parental self-esteem simply boils down to this: *one of the best ways to foster positive self-esteem in their child is for parents to consistently nurture it within themselves.*

6

SIMILARITY AND SELF-ESTEEM

THE "GOOD" CHILD AND THE "BAD"

From the outset of life, social pressure on the child to conform begins at home, as parents—the principal caretakers, the primary companions, the earliest playmates, and the resident powers that be—set the family terms on which the little boy or girl must live. To win approval, have wants met, and often receive expressions of love, the child learns that it helps to fit in and go along. The *psychology of similarity* causes the boy or girl to strive to be like the people who run the family system in order to be liked, and to get what he or she likes, in return.

The child discovers that similarity to those who govern the family system (and to authorities who run other social systems later on) tends to be rewarded: "The more I act like them and how they want me to, the better I get treated." As for parents, *their "easiest" child is usually the one who is most similar to them.* The exception to this statement is where similarity conflicts arise, such as a parent fighting to change in his child (procrastination, for example) what he has never been able to change in himself.

Like other social animals, however, human beings tend to take comfort and safety from similarity, and tend to experience more discomfort and danger around diversity. So a child's similarity to them can create a sense of familiarity and compatibility. "We've never had a day of trouble with our child. She likes what we like and acts like we want." Unchosen resemblance of the inherited kind (genetic similarity of valued traits of personality, temperament, intelligence, or physical appearance) often enhances sense of similarity even further, just as lack of genetic similarity (in step-relationships or adoption, for example) can reduce resemblance and create more unfamiliarity to get used to.

The Child Who Is "Different"

Because similarity to parents is so often rewarded with their approval, it tends to support a child's self-esteem. When the child's self-definition mirrors much of the parents' image, parents are often pleased to see so much of themselves reflected in their child. But what happens when there is significant diversity between parents and child instead? What happens when their respective human natures do not match, with each party in the relationship struggling with fundamental differences between them?

Suppose the following family scenario unfolds. Firstborn child is strongly built like both parents, is also socially outspoken and outgoing, and has the same high-energy level and natural athletic capacity. In addition, *child number one* is eager to learn game-playing skills from parents, enjoys their outdoor interests, is generally compliant to their wishes, and assimilates their devotion to watching and participating in all manner of popular sports. Together all three make up a mutual admiration society in which part of the pleasure of their company is the sense of sharing so much in common with each other.

Then along comes *child number two*, who from the outset appears *different* from child number one. Frail and reflective, slower to physically develop, easily tired, favoring indoors over outdoors, preferring reading and fantasizing to playing games or spectating sports, inward and less communicative, and stubborn and resistant when asked or told to interrupt concentrated solitary play.

Comparisons Can Be Destructive

It isn't that the parents love child number two less than child number one, but they do agree that number two "is our difficult child," not "easy" like number one, a judgment that becomes more strongly felt when number two follows number one into adolescence. "Our first is talkative with us, willing to do what we want and fun to be with, but our second prefers being alone, and fights us when we want him to join in and go along. He doesn't want to be part of family activities, and we find his friends and interests very difficult to understand. He insists on being different. And when we've had all the differentness we can take, we can end up criticizing and correcting him a lot of times, trying to get him to be more like the rest of us."

If similarity to the parental values and norms tends to be rewarded with approval, a child's differentness is sometimes penalized with lack of parental understanding and acceptance, with parental frustration with nonconformity, with conflict over noncompliance, even with anger at the child's stubborn defiance to remain unchanged. "Get used to it! I'm not like both of you and my sister, and I'm not going to be!"

For the different child, not fitting into the dominant family culture can feel lonely and disapproved, on both counts hard on the child's self-esteem. Every message to change feels like one more experience of rejection.

The Evaluative Trap

When parents judge one child "easy" based on similarity to themselves and another "hard" based on diverging from the family norm, they are in danger of beginning a chain of evaluation that can lead to equating easy with "good," and difficult with "bad." From this distinction, an appearance of preference (prejudice) and favoritism (discrimination) can arise. The good child receives more positive reviews and rewards, whereas the bad child receives less of each.

In the extreme, feeling unfairly treated by this inequity, the bad child may act out in anger at this perceived unfairness, increasing his or her negative reputation and treatment, becoming a lightning rod for conflict in the family, and monopolizing a lot of parental concern. Meanwhile, the good child keeps accumulating praise and reaping benefits that parents have to offer.

These contrasting roles played by each child often gives rise to jealously between them. The difficult child envies the disproportionate amount of parental approval the easy child receives. The easy child envies the greater amount of parental time devoted to the difficult child. As for the parents, they are not meaning to be unfair. They are usually just trying their best to "straighten" the bad child out by reforming him into meeting their definition of "good."

Rewarding Similarity Can Damage "Bad" Child and "Good"

Parents need to beware rewarding similarity too much because it cannot only injure the "bad" child's self-esteem, it can also harm the self-esteem of the "good." How? Consider what can happen at the end of adolescence. Then, departing into independence, the "bad" child can honestly claim the individuality for which he or she has always fought. As for parents, at last out of the business of active parenting, they may finally give up the battle and accept their more difficult child for who and how he or she is. Now they are able to appreciate the good in the difficult child because they no longer feel obliged to change the bad.

Child number one, however, the good child since the beginning, may be left with a serious problem. To preserve this positive reputation all these years, some authenticity may have been sacrificed to keep earning a positive parental evaluation. To please parents or to avoid the kind of criticism and conflict the younger child has received, child number one may have suppressed his or her different or difficult side. Thus, on the threshold of true independence, the good child feels trapped, committed to maintaining an ideal image for fear of breaking it and losing standing in parental eyes: "I couldn't bear disappointing them!" *When a person denies himself or herself authenticity for the sake of similarity to significant others, this suppression of honest individuality may diminish self-esteem: "I hate feeling unable to be the person I really am."*

The bad part of being the "bad" child is disapproval received for being different from parents. "How am I supposed to feel good about myself when my parents don't like the way I am?" The bad part of being the "good" child is the constant pressure to remain similar to parents to keep winning their approval. "How am I supposed to feel good about myself when I can't afford to let my parents know a lot about how I really am?"

To help keep from falling into either trap of "good" child or "bad," parents can treat both similarity and diversity within the family as part of the human mix to which every child is entitled. To grow into the fullness of how one truly is, each child needs room to act both easy and difficult, sometimes good child and sometimes bad. *Self-esteem partly depends on being valued for being similar to parents, and partly on being valued for being different.*

7

COMMUNICATION

SPEAKING UP TO OTHERS

How a child manages the spoken word can have a profound effect on his or her self-esteem. Communication is a process of sending verbal messages describing something about oneself to others, and in the process *socially defining* who and how one is. Such self-definition is one of the two components of self-esteem.

Communication as an Act of Speaking Up

Other people, even those we love, must depend upon adequate and accurate information from us to know what we are *feeling*, are *thinking*, and have been *doing*. Relying on sources other than ourselves for any of this personal data amounts to gossip at worst and hearsay at best. The same dependency holds for us in knowing them. This is why *a major responsibility* each party has in a relationship is for self-definition, *for being known* by the other party.

"But," protests the child, "if you really loved me, I wouldn't have to explain for you to know how I feel!" No. Love only increases the desire to know. A person can guess, empathize, intuit, and imagine, but only by being told can one be truly informed. *People cannot read each other's minds.*

So, how is verbal communication transmitted? By a person *speaking up* in at least five different ways.

1. Speaking up lets a person *express* the thoughts and feeling that make up his or her inner experience.

Asked about how school was, the child replies: "I didn't get chosen by either team at recess and it really hurt my feelings." *Talking out hard experience with someone else allows a person to feel acknowledged and supported.*

2. Speaking up lets a person *explain* opinions and beliefs in order to declare his or her view. Commenting on unhappiness in a friend's family, the child says: "I think it's wrong for parents to divorce!" *Sharing opinions and beliefs with someone else allows a person to have his or her position understood.*

3. Speaking up lets a person *question* in order to understand what is happening, asking to find out. A change in the parent's life causes the child to want to know: "Are we going to be all right now that you've been laid off from your job?" *Requesting information from someone else can allow a person to get answers that reduce anxiety from ignorance.*

4. Speaking up lets a person *confront* unacceptable treatment by taking stands when he or she feels wronged. "It's not fair when you make one of us do chores and let the other get away with doing none!" *Objecting to what feels unjust from someone else allows a person to take up for his or her self-interest.*

5. Speaking up lets a person *resolve* disagreements with others. "I want to find a solution that works for both of us." *Being willing to discuss an honest difference with someone else allows a person to work out conflicts with others.*

Through all five ways of speaking up—expressing, explaining, questioning, confronting, and resolving—a child honors his or her responsibility for being known by others. For this communication to occur, the child must hold himself or herself in enough esteem to *risk* becoming socially defined as an individual.

What are the risks?

- Of self-exposure and perhaps experiencing embarrassment
- Of being insensitive and perhaps causing injury
- Of offending and perhaps arousing disapproval
- Of creating disagreement and perhaps inciting conflict
- Of alienating others and perhaps receiving rejection
- Of appearing too different and perhaps becoming excluded

It often takes courage to speak up, braving social responses one does not control, daring to be known. *The willingness to speak up, to be socially outspoken, both depends on, and can nourish, self-esteem.* The alternative to speaking up, *shutting up*, often reflects a lack of (and can lower) self-esteem.

The Perils of Shutting Up

The legacy of learning to speak up in one's family of origin usually empowers children to be socially outspoken in adolescent and later adult relationships. Unhappily, the opposite legacy may afflict those children who grow up in a family where speaking up is not modeled, encouraged, or allowed, or perhaps is not safe. In consequence, *habits of shutting up* may be learned. At worst, these habits can inhibit social definition and diminish self-esteem.

- Rather than learning to express their inner experience, children may learn to withhold and withdraw, to remain *silent* instead.
- Rather than learning to voice their opinions and beliefs, children may learn to defer to the views of others and remain *undeclared* instead.

- Rather than learning to question to find out, children may learn to *wait to be told* (or not be told) instead.
- Rather than learning to assert themselves and object to unacceptable treatment, children may learn to passively *accept any treatment* given instead.
- Rather than learning to contest significant differences, children may learn to concede and *avoid conflict* instead.

In consequence of this education in shutting up, not only can children refrain from social self-definition and diminish self-esteem, they can become *socially compliant* to their costs, in danger of living too much on other people's terms and not enough on their own. In the extreme, this social compliance can leave children undefended and vulnerable to *exploitation* (repeatedly letting themselves be taken advantage of) and *victimization* (repeatedly letting themselves be hurt).

Encouraging Speaking Up

To encourage speaking up, there are three simple steps parents can take.

1. *Model speaking up.* (Parents who routinely talk about their thoughts and feelings often have children who learn to do the same for themselves.)

2. *Support speaking up.* (Parents who take the time to pay attention to speaking up by listening with interest often have children who value being known.)

3. *Keep speaking up safe.* (Parents who are careful to refrain from criticism, ridicule, or sarcasm in response to their son's or daughter's communication often have children who have no fear of speaking up.)

Of course, children must be taught some guidelines for speaking up, doing it in such a way that they do not dominate all communication (being unwilling "to share the stage," for example) or say things that have an abusive effect (using language with deliberate intent to hurt, for example).

Discouraging Shutting Up

To discourage *a shy son or daughter* from continually shutting up, parents cannot literally force communication out of the child. They can, however, *hold the child responsible for refusing to be known*, explaining the consequences that shutting up can create.

- "If you don't *express* your emotions, then I can't know what's going on inside you, so I may act unmindfully of how you feel."
- "If you don't *explain* your point of view, then I can't know what you think, and so may assume you have no strong opinion either way."
- "If you don't *ask*, then I can't know what you need to know, and so may not be able to give you information you need to understand."
- "If you don't *confront* me when you feel I'm mistreating you, then I can't know when my actions are offensive, and so may not change what you wish I would correct."
- "If you don't *disagree* with me over some difference between us, then I can't know we are in conflict, and so may not be able to work out the issue you would like resolved."

The shy child is a shutting up child who sacrifices self-esteem by shying away from social self-definition. Peers sometimes think this noncommunication is the behavior of a snob acting superior by refusing to talk, which is one way shy children are commonly misunderstood.

Although, given the choice, some parents may prefer having a socially compliant child to having a socially outspoken one, *in general, speaking up and the social definition it creates, supports far more self-esteem among children than does shutting up.*

A parent can tell a socially compliant child something like this: "There's nothing wrong with feeling shy, but acting shy will only make those feelings worse." At the same time, the mother or father also needs to appreciate and compliment one shutting up skill of great value that many shy children possess: Often they have learned to *listen* extremely well.

8

COURTESY

LITTLE THINGS MEAN A LOT

At the end of the day, an elementary teacher takes time to ask students to discuss any painful ways they were treated by her or by other students that seemed too small to speak up about at the time, but hurt too much to ignore and are still remembered. A sampling of responses to her question sounds like this.

- "You wouldn't call on me when I had something to say."
- "I gave my friend a pencil and she didn't even say thanks."
- "Nobody noticed the artwork I made today."
- "He cut in front of me in line without asking."
- "I got laughed at when I was being serious."
- "Nobody saved me a place to sit at the lunch table."
- "Yesterday my friend borrowed fifty cents, and today forgot to pay it back."
- "When I started to talk, other people interrupted."
- "I gave my ideas, but nobody listened."
- "At recess, no one threw the ball to me."

Small Is Big

What is the teacher getting at by discussing such little things? *Discourtesy* is the answer—*those small daily acts of insensitivity that signify something very large—lack of caring and consideration and respect for other people.* She wants the children to appreciate the power of *courtesy* in their treatment of each other.

Courtesy includes many small acts of consideration that can mean a lot. Being listened to, for example, may feel like being treated as though one has something *worth* saying. *Listening can signify interest.* Having a piece of artwork complimented, for example, may feel like being treated as though what one accomplished is *worth* valuing. *Compliments can signify approval.* Being thanked for doing someone a favor, for example, may feel like being treated as though one is *worth* being given gratitude. *Being thanked can signify appreciation.*

By the same token, not to be listened to can feel like *neglect.* Not to be complimented can feel like *rejection.* Not to be thanked can feel like *being taken for granted.* This is the teacher's point: small acts of consideration that all students can identify signify a lot when they are given and when they are withheld. Because such consideration can encourage people to feel good about themselves when it is given and feel bad about themselves when it is not, *courteous treatment has a major impact on self-esteem.* Most important, treating each other with courtesy is something everyone can *choose* to do.

How Courtesy Counts at Home

What holds true for school holds even more powerfully at home. The small courtesies family members show each other contribute enormously to the quality of their family life. Certainly coping well with big things like conflict, change, and crisis is important to everybody's welfare, but these challenges are occasional, whereas the little moment-to-moment choices about how to treat each other have constant impact on everybody's sense of self-esteem.

In being respected by their parents in small ways, children not only feel good about themselves at the time, they also are encouraged to place value on their own self-worth, because they are *worth* treating well. *How children are treated has a lot to do with how they learn to treat themselves and to treat others in return.*

Big Things Are Not Enough

Parents who believe that providing big things for their children should be enough, are often mistaken. Self-preoccupied when not engaged in parenting, or impatient and demanding when so involved, they may ignore showing everyday consideration, reserving such expressions of sensitivity for special occasions. Unwittingly, they send a potentially hurtful message: unless the occasion is sufficiently special, the child is usually not worth treating well. "Why can't you be as nice to me on other days as you are on my birthday?"

Or, consider this scenario: At the supper table, a tired parent, weary of dealing patiently with complaining people all day, keeps criticizing the children for irritating table manners and for mumbling instead of speaking up. Then the telephone rings, and the parent answers with a sudden change of attitude, becoming warm and friendly, good humored and helpful. "Who was that?" asks a child after the parent has hung up. "I don't know," the answer snaps back. "Somebody new at work. Now eat your food, and stop dawdling!" That's when the child asks another, more telling question: "How come you treat a stranger nicer than you treat us? Who matters more?"

Sometimes parents get in the habit of treating outside relationships, particularly those at their job, with more courtesy than they give their children at home. Yet, work relationships are only contractual, services sold in return for money, whereas family relationships are a matter of love. Hopefully, the parent who received this child's question will be given pause to think.

Modeling and Instruction—Making Courtesy a Two-way Street

Parents who want to be treated with consideration by their child need *to model* that show of consideration themselves. Thus, after an hour of repeatedly nagging the thirteen-year-old to pick up the bedroom, the task is finally accomplished. Although inclined by frustration with delay to grumble, "Well it's about time!" the parent responds with courtesy instead. "Thank you for cleaning up. Your room looks nice." Appreciation and a compliment from a tired parent, whose insistence has at last worn down adolescent resistance, affirms the child for doing what was asked.

Parents who want to be treated with consideration by their child also need *to instruct* in common courtesies that matter to them. Thus, when a child thoughtlessly borrows a belonging from them without permission, they let the child know that taking without asking feels like a lack of respect. In the future, they want the courtesy of a request, and the child complies.

Through modeling and instruction of courtesy in the family, parents can make clear to children that in their routine daily treatment of each other, little things can mean a lot to everyone's self-esteem.

9

CONFLICT

FIGHTING TO PRESERVE SELF-ESTEEM

Conflict is *not* a sign of something wrong in a relationship. It is *not* a problem. It is a functional process that allows people to identify, encounter, and resolve inevitable human differences that arise between them. In families, conflicts are built into the dynamics of daily life in the form of questions, the answers to which are continually being contested.

- Parents can disagree with each other over *cooperation.* Who does what role? How are supervisory responsibilities going to be shared?
- Parents can disagree with children over *control.* Who gets to decide the rules? Whose way is the right way?
- Children can disagree with each other over *competition.* Who goes first? Who gets most?
- Children can disagree with parents over *conformity.* Who has to live on whose lifestyle terms? To what degree should fitting into the family be required?

As long as individual human differences exist, and they always will, conflict between family members is not going to go away. Therefore, because some conflict is unavoidable, parents need to consider "*How* is it to be conducted?" The healthy answer is: "In ways that do no injury to anyone's self-esteem."

How the Conduct of Conflict Can Hurt Self-Esteem

Conflict can be an emotionally arousing experience when it causes *frustration* from opposition, *anger* from frustration, and even *fear* of anger. When any of these emotions dictate what is said and done in conflict, momentary impulse can cause a person to inflict serious injury to the opponent's self-esteem. *In family conflicts where emotion is unrestrained, impulse can rule to destructive effect.*

Any time one family member verbally or physically attacks another in conflict with intent to win at all costs or to hurt that person, a fundamental trust is broken—*trust in safety guaranteed by love.* As long as family members act out of love for each other, caring causes them not to want to do each other harm. In conflict, however, driven by momentary upset, people can lose touch with caring feelings and behave in destructive ways.

For people in general, and for children in particular, love from those whose love they value most of all—like parents—is a vital source of self-esteem: "I feel good about myself because my parents love me." Temporary loss of love's assurance, shown by loss of parental caring in conflict, can come as an enormous blow: "It really hurt to have you hit me and say you wish you'd never had me!"

To be injured in this fashion can harm both sources of a child's self-esteem. Self-definition can be hurt: "I have lost my parent's love." Self-evaluation can be hurt: "I'm no longer worth my parent's love." After calming down and realizing the damage that was inflicted by angry action and angry speech, the parent may apologize and attempt to undo what was done. History, however, has a long memory, and once spoken, words cannot be actually retracted anymore than the sting from a slap can be taken away.

Between parents and children:

- Differences are inevitable
- Conflict is unavoidable
- But *violence is neither*

Because the conduct of conflict is a matter of choice, that conduct can be controlled. It is up to parents to set the example, give the instruction, and enforce the standards for conducting conflict in ways that respect everyone's self-esteem. They can do this by remembering that conflict is not something they happen to *have* with their children, but is something they purposely *do* with their children. It is intentional, not accidental. And it is cooperative—it takes two to make a conflict, but only one to stop it. "Suppose they gave a war and nobody, or only one side, came?" Both the creation and conduct of conflict are matters over which family members have responsible choice.

As for preventing violence, physical restraint is the easy part because most family violence is not of the physical kind. Remember this riddle: "When in conflict, what do humans and most other animals have in common?" Answer: "They all fight with their mouths." The old adage that "sticks and stones can break my bones but words can never hurt me" is simply untrue. Angry words are the most common weapon of choice in human conflict, and in family conflict they cause most of the damage. As emotional intensity escalates, hurtful words are more likely to be called upon to defend one's position or to attack the other's. So there need to be some family rules for keeping the conduct of conflict within respectful limits.

Rules for Fighting that Help Preserve Self-Esteem

1. *Keeping priorities clear*. Because conflict can be an emotionally arousing experience, *the first priority*

is not resolving the issue at difference, but rather *both parties monitoring their own emotional intensity*, keeping it in check so judgment, not impulse, rules the interaction. The process is always more important than the outcome because preserving an ongoing loving bond is at stake. To win an argument by damaging the opposing family member is ultimately self-destructive because some trust in the relationship, for the injured party at least, has now been lost.

2. *Safety first.* Conflict is never to be used as an excuse for doing another family member any kind of harm. Family conflict is only intended for clarifying differences and working out disagreements in such a way that no one gets hurt.

3. *Violation agreement.* Should anyone, in the course of conflict, feel threatened or injured as a consequence of what the other person said or did, then the issue at difference is to be set aside. The violation of safety needs to be given top priority, to be discussed, and to be corrected before returning to the original issue at difference.

4. *Separation and return.* In monitoring one's own emotional arousal, if either party feels in danger of "losing it" and doing or saying something he or she may have later cause to regret, that person shall have the *right* to separate and cool down. Along with this right, however, is accepting the *responsibility* for setting a mutually agreed upon time to return to working on resolving the conflict after emotional sobriety has been restored.

5. *Loyalty.* Because frustration and anger in conflict can be the momentary enemy of loving feelings,

clear reassurance must be given that no disagreement will break anyone's commitment of caring or cause either person to abandon the relationship.

6. *Speaking up and shutting up.* No matter how well both parties know each other, there can be no mind reading about what the other person feels or thinks or wants. Each person is responsible for *speaking up* and making his or her own experience, desires, and opinions known. With this responsibility goes another, for *shutting up* and listening when the other person is talking, making every effort to understand the opposing view without closing down because one's mind is already made up.

7. *No name-calling.* Because frustration in conflict tends to encourage people to become more abstract in their use of language and to become less specific, it is easy to get into name-calling. "You're not being *sensible!*" "Well, you're not being *respectful!*" Rather than engage in such insults, it is better to stick to the specifics of the disagreement: what exactly is it that each party wants or does not want to have happen? Never resolving a conflict, name-calling only inflames it.

8. *No laughing matter.* Challenging a parent over a difference, the child puts his or her self-esteem at stake by going up against such a powerful adult. Therefore, parents need to treat conflict with a child as a serious matter, and not intentionally or nervously smile or laugh. To do so risks leaving the child feeling discounted and put down, humiliated and angry.

9. *No meltdowns.* Because conflict creates resemblance, with both parties drawn to use the other party's effective tactics against them, each person

should model those constructive behaviors he or she wants to deal with in return. Neither party should be drawn into imitating destructive behavior just because that is what the other is doing. Instead, issue should be taken with that conduct directly or as part of the violation agreement.

10. *No carryovers.* If as a function of a previous conflict either party carries forward unresolved grievance ("I'm still angry from the last fight") or anxiety ("I'm scared about the next fight"), then air that grievance or anxiety before allowing it to intensify the next disagreement.

11. *Goal of intimacy.* Treat conflict as an opportunity to get to know the other person better, and to become better known by the other person, from working through human differences in the relationship. Treat differences not as barriers to keep people apart, but as bridges creating understandings and agreements that can tie both parties more closely together.

10

CORRECTION

CHOICES AND CONSEQUENCES

To be corrected by parents for one's misbehavior can be hard on a child's self-esteem because it means bearing disapproval from those the boy or girl wants most to please. Like conflict, however, some parental discipline is unavoidable because mistakes, misadventures, and misdeeds are all part of the trial-and-error process of growing up.

To channel or redirect a child's growth, sometimes parents are required to assert *authority* (taking firm stands about what needs to happen) or to administer various forms of *correction* (using management techniques to influence behavior), both of which the child may not like.

Parents *assert authority* by:

- Setting limits: "You can't do that."
- Making demands: "You have to do this."
- Asking questions: "Where have you been?"
- Confronting to discuss: "Tell us what happened."
- Taking value positions: "This is right and that is wrong."

Parents commonly *correct behavior* by exercising influence in four ways. If the child is susceptible to verbal explanation or instruction, numbers one and two often prove sufficient. If actions must be found to speak louder than words, then numbers three and four may be required.

1. *Guidance* is the power of persuasion. Here, parents provide reasons about why the child's behavior is unacceptable and how it needs to change. *Effective parents are relentless communicators (allowing children to always know where they stand).*

2. *Supervision* is the power of insistence. Here, parents repeat and repeat what it is they want until they wear resistance down and the child finally complies. *Effective parents are persistent naggers (and nagging is honorable work—it shows that parents will not give up when an issue needs to be addressed).*

3. *Structure* is the power of enforcing rules by punishing violations. Here, parents set the boundaries for acceptable behavior, and when the child goes outside those boundaries, a consequence is applied (usually freedom taken away or extra work given) to cause the offender to reconsider making the same bad choice another time. *Effective parents keep punishment constructive (making sure the consequence is relevant to the offense).*

4. *Working the exchange points* is the power of exploiting the child's dependency upon the parents. Here, parents withhold or delay giving what the child wants from them until they are given what they requested first. *Effective parents insist on an adequate exchange (so that the child is taught to contribute effort and cooperate with them just as they do with the child).*

"Preaching," "bugging me," "power trips," and "blackmail" are the disparaging terms given to these thankless acts of corrective parenting by children who usually do not appreciate such contributions to their welfare at the time.

Because parenting is not a popularity contest, however, *sometimes taking stands for the child's best interests against what he or she may want is just part of being a responsible mother and father.*

Patience and persistence are also required. Because *most children* (and adults) *are not one-trial learners* when it comes to changing their behavior, to modify inappropriate or unruly conduct often requires repeat corrections over time. This is not a problem for parents to get upset about, but a reality they need to accept. "Why can't you remember after the first time you are told?" they will often ask the child in frustration. Because many times, more than once is required.

Correction Is Criticism Enough

To be corrected to any degree by parents indicates that the child knowingly or unknowingly is behaving in some way they disapprove, so *criticism is implicit in correction.* They don't like something about how the child is choosing to act (doing a chore incompletely, not keeping an agreement, breaking a rule, for example) and they want it stopped or improved.

Correction communicates rejection: "We don't accept your conduct and we want it changed." Hopefully, the child understands that this rejection applies only to the behavior, not to the person. To help the child keep in mind this distinction, they may couple correction with an assurance: "Just because we don't like how you're acting doesn't mean that we don't still like and love who you are."

What parents must keep in mind is that any expression of their disapproval, correction being a common one, threatens the evaluation component of their child's self-esteem, which partly depends on maintaining a good reputation with parents. Therefore, *adding personal criticism to correction only creates a double jeopardy for the child.*

For example, angry at the child's misbehavior, there are certain statements parents have been known to make that can do crushing damage to the child's self-esteem: "I'm so disappointed in you!" "We'll never forgive you!" "You should be ashamed of yourself!"

Each of these blanket condemnations threatens an irrecoverable loss of standing in parental eyes. That loss immeasurably diminishes the child's self-esteem. "My parents have lost all respect for me. I just hate myself for what I did!" *Most parental criticism is not a good corrective because provoking someone to feel bad about themselves does not usually motivate them to do better* ("And we'll keep criticizing until your attitude improves!"). Specific opposition is usually more effective than general disapproval: "We really disagree with your decision, here is why, and to remind you to choose differently the next time, there will be a consequence to work off the offense."

The Building Blocks of Cooperation

Parents tend to correct when they are not getting the cooperation from the child they want. Thus, somewhere around the age of three, parents can begin putting the following building blocks for cooperation into place. *Listening and attending:* "What did you hear me say?" *Anticipating and predicting:* "What will happen if you make that choice?" *Agreement and commitment:* "What did you promise me you would do?" *Helping and chores:* "What do you need to get done for me before I do for you?" *The more cooperation parents teach, the less reliant on correction they become.*

Constructive Correction

"Don't do that!" "Stop it!" "That's no way to act!" These three common statements of correction are usually given by frustrated parents to get the child to quit some offensive or even dangerous behavior. At best, however, these commands are only partially effective. The urgency with which they are spoken certainly communicates disapproval, but the boy or girl is only left with a vague understanding of doing something "wrong."

A negative command has little instructional power. Far more effective is to follow the cease and desist order with:

- An *explanation* ("Here is *why* I am asking you to stop.")
- A *positive alternative* ("Rather than doing it that way, let me suggest another way *instead.*")
- A *specific direction* ("Here is how it can be safely done.")
- A *rewarding response* ("Good for you, you did it right!")

Neutralizing Correction

One way to soften the critical impact of correction is to describe correction as a process in which both parent and child have responsibility. To begin, parents can declare that correction is *not* a part of parenting they enjoy. It causes them to express disapproval of the child's actions and, if consequences are applied, to place a strain on their relationship. They are not doing this negative thing to the child, but *for the child;* not to hurt the child, but *to help the child;* not to enjoy power over the child, but *to risk unpopularity with the child* for his or her welfare. All this they are doing because one part of their parental responsibility is to help shape their child's growth by influencing the decisions he or she makes, supporting the good and opposing the bad, taking responsibility for making that evaluation.

Then they can explain how correction is a shared responsibility.

1. "*We* have control over deciding the rules by which you live as long as you live with us."

2. "*You* have control over deciding to live within those rules or not."
3. "*We* have control over deciding consequences when those rules are kept and broken."
4. "*You* have control over getting positive consequences and avoiding negative consequences by obeying our rules and thus living free of correction."

For the child, to feel in control of the consequences one receives can be a powerful enhancement of self-esteem: "I can choose to get a lot of what I want."

After any correction has been given and the child has complied with the consequences, parents make sure to *normalize* his or her standing in the relationship: "We appreciate how you dealt with the consequences and we will not bring this problem up again. You have paid for what is past. We want you to know that we think as well of you as always, that we have as much faith in you as always, and of course that we love you as much as always." Notice the *courtesy* (positive notice) that parents give. They *thank* the child for working with them to work off the offense, positively recognizing both cooperation that has been given and the restitution that has been made. Completing successful restitution can enhance self-esteem: "I did what it took to make up for my wrong."

The Most Powerful Consequence of All

As trainers of trick-performing animals have proven through practice for years, the most powerful way to shape a fellow creature's behavior in the direction the trainer wants is *not* simply by applying punishing consequences for doing wrong, but through giving rewarding consequences for doing right. This approach also works in parenting. A smile from a parent for doing well can have far more shaping influence than a spank for doing badly. Why?

Human beings are reward-seeking creatures. Most of what they do is motivated by the desire to get what they want. *Punishments teach people about what not to do* by injuring their well-being. *Rewards teach people how to do* by encouraging learning. *Rewards reinforce self-esteem* (feeling good about oneself), whereas punishment reduces self-esteem (feeling bad about oneself). Given the choice, most children prefer treatment that enhances rather than diminishes good feelings about themselves.

The watchword for parents is:

- Don't commit to punishment as the most powerful source of parental influence.
- Don't focus entirely on problems and ignore what is going well.
- Don't take the positive for granted, but recognize and reward it with attention when it occurs.

Remember the example of animals trainers, continually shaping behavior by consistently rewarding choices they want the creature to make. Parental rewards need not be material in nature. Indeed, *relational rewards are the most powerful of all.* Because most children want to "shine" in their parent's eyes, acts of parental acceptance, attention, appreciation, affection, approval, and praise all reinforce positive behavior and affirm a child's self-esteem.

11

HELPING

GIVING ASSISTANCE CAN ENHANCE SELF-ESTEEM

How is a child different from an adolescent? One common way is in the eagerness to help at home when asked. The four-year-old tends to welcome helping a parent as an opportunity to act grown up. "Can I help now?" begs the little child, impatient to contribute. The fourteen-year-old, however, is more likely to spurn the invitation, treating it instead as an adult imposition on his or her free time. "Can't I do it later?" the adolescent complains.

There is a lesson in this example. If parents want to have a helpful teenager, they'd better start laying the groundwork long before adolescent *resistance to assistance* sets in (between ages 9 and 13). *Habituate the child to household helping early, and cooperation is more likely later on.* By age three, a child can begin giving simple assistance—picking up, putting back, and lending a hand with straightening up around the home.

Because the relationship between children and helping has a lot to do with building self-esteem, parents need to understand exactly how this connection works.

Helping as an Act of Power

The key to unlocking the complexity of helping is to understand that this common human act is not so much a service or support to be given as it is a *power* to be exercised. Think of it this way: people do not request or accept help *unless* they perceive that the helper has some power to do for them what they cannot do or do not want to do for themselves. Or at least they believe that the helper can pitch in on what they wish to accomplish.

When a child asks a parent: "Can I help?" the boy or girl is not only wanting to keep the adult company, he or she is also looking for an opportunity to exercise some helping power. Why? Because to have one's help accepted is to be recognized as a person who has something of value to offer. *Helping enhances self-esteem by affirming one's power to be beneficial to someone else: "When I can help other people, I feel good about myself because I have something worthwhile to offer."*

The Payoffs of Helping

Examples of how giving help helps build a child's self-esteem are endless. There is the older child who has something *worth* teaching a younger child. There is the little child whose small size is *worth* a lot when he or she can crawl into a narrow space and retrieve what a parent is too large to reach. There is the child whose comforting words are *worth* a lot to an unhappy older sibling who feels down and lonely from a hard day at school. There is the adolescent on a church mission trip whose labor is *worth* enough to help construct housing for people in need of shelter. There is even the sullenly obedient teenager who really didn't want to join in painting the family home, but afterward feels *proud* of what he or she helped accomplish.

If possible, when a child asks to help, parents should try to welcome the offer of assistance. This is not always easy when unskilled help is neither efficient nor convenient. In addition, parents may be pressed for time, concerned about quality of task performance, or simply want to enjoy doing the job themselves. But the child is blissfully unaware of the sacrifices that parents are being asked to make. "Can I help spread the frosting on the cake? I've never done that before." It's tempting for parents to respond: "You'll make more work; you don't know how; you'll do it wrong." *Reject the young child's desire to help, however, and parents miss out on a chance to enhance his or her self-esteem and possibly lose out on obtaining willing help from a teenager later on.*

Social Value and Self-Esteem

Parents who refuse to let a child help or who refuse to ask a child for help (in either case insisting on doing all the work themselves) diminish the child's opportunity to exercise helping power and the affirmation of self-worth it brings. Carried to an extreme, perhaps *a child who has been able to help a lot* grows up feeling "good for something," whereas *a child who has never been allowed to help* grows up feeling "good for nothing."

This latter phrase is worth considering. Did you ever hear a young person being called a "*good for nothing?*" Did you ever stop to think about what a devastating judgment that is? What degree of self-esteem can a child have who is considered, and who thus considers himself or herself "good for nothing?" The answer is: *pretty low*. So, to encourage self-esteem through being of help, have your child help around the home, or volunteer in the community, through your church, or through service-learning projects at his or her school. *To feel "good for something" is good for self-esteem.*

Self-Help and Self-Esteem

Not only does it feel affirming and empowering to help others, it also feels affirming and empowering to help oneself. *Self-esteem from self-reliance is the result.* Independence and self-sufficiency depend on one's capacity to help oneself. Thus, to a degree, all parental help can interfere with the child learning to help himself or herself.

Sometimes in consequence of parental help, the child's dependency may be fostered and self-sufficiency may actually be diminished.

Of course, when their child is in trouble or has a problem, it is natural for parents to want to help. But if by rushing in and giving help to their child they reduce the child's opportunity for self-help, what are parents supposed to do? The answer is: whenever they want to give help, they should do so by keeping their child's self-esteem from self-reliance in mind. And they can act on this principle by *teaching*, by *contracting*, and by *refusal.*

- *Teaching.* If the child doesn't know how to do something that needs to be done, then as part of the help they give, parents can give instruction so the next time the child is in a better position to help herself.
- *Contracting.* If the child wants help with a problem, parents can decide not to help too much. They can say to the child: "We will do this part of the help you need, and you can do the rest by yourself."
- *Refusal.* If the child wants help to get out of a difficulty he has chosen to get into, perhaps having made the same unwise choice before, parents may want to give the hardest help of all: the refusal to help. "We believe you had what it took to choose your way into this problem, and we believe you have what it takes to choose your way out."

12

MONEY

CAN SELF-ESTEEM BE BOUGHT?

In a materialistic society like the United States, where advertising, the media, and the marketplace all conspire to encourage young people to want more goods and life experiences than are required to meet their basic needs, a child's buying power becomes a kind of social power. How? Because the amount of money spent on a child, and the amount of money a child has to spend, has consequences on his or her definition of self, evaluation of self, relationship with peers, and degree of personal choice.

As fitting in, belonging to, and keeping up with a group of friends become increasingly important, particularly during the adolescent years, money comes to matter a lot because it helps determine what one can afford *to see* (entertainment), can afford *to do* (recreation), and can afford *to have* (possessions). For example, whether or not one has the money to go to concerts with friends, to play league sports with friends, and to wear a certain fashion in clothes like friends can all influence the company a child chooses to keep, or the decision of others to socially include that child. No wonder most young people in this country partly link their self-esteem to the material goods and worldly experiences money can buy.

Consider several ways money can matter in the life of a child.

1. As *a means of exchange* that can be traded for material

goods and worldly experiences, money can be used both to satisfy wants and enhance **self-image**. "I like the way I look wearing this style of clothes."

2. As *a measure of personal value*, money can confer social status by equating degree of material abundance with **self-worth**. "People know I can afford the best, and I like that."
3. As *a manner of acquisition*, how money is obtained can contribute to **self-respect**. "I'm proud to have earned the money to buy my car."

Money and Self-Image

Even adults know that possessions make a personal statement about the possessor, or why else would they care about what they wear, where they live, what they drive, and what else they own? Material belongings express something about the person, creating an image for the world to see.

For adolescents insecurely searching for identity as they grow, hungry for peer acceptance all the while, the issue of *image* becomes very important. To be in search of identity and acceptance is to be at an impressionable age, and this vulnerability in young people is relentlessly exploited by how most every youth product is promoted—by creating a desirable social image that goes with it. The implied promise is: *buy the product and the image will be yours.*

What image? For teenagers, it is usually some combination of *confident* young people, looking *attractive,* acting *sexy*, feeling *excited*, having *fun*, being *popular*, using the product to *feel good about themselves*. Because many hundreds of commercial messages sell the same underlying image to children every day, no wonder young people come to believe in the materialism they are sold. "Happiness depends on what you have." "What you have is who you are."

"Not to have what others have is to be socially *out of it.*"

For parents, the challenge here is to help the child develop a positive self-image that is not primarily dependent on having the "in" things that money can buy. To do so requires parents to try to clarify common confusions by offering an *independent perspective.*

- Despite what children are led to believe, *image is not the same as reality:* "When you buy something, all you get is the product; the image is just created to get the product sold."
- Despite what children are led to believe, *things are not what make a person:* "Possessions do not make you who you are; they're just objects that you own."
- Despite what children are led to believe, *buying something is not the same as bettering oneself:* "At most, buying can add another thing to what you have, but it can never improve the actual person that you are."

Money and Self-Worth

Almost every child in the United States, no matter how economically advantaged, grows up materially deprived. How can this be? Because certain *realities of our consumer life* make it so.

1. Fads and fashions change too fast for any child to keep up with them all.
2. There are too many products for any child to afford them all.
3. There is always someone a child knows who has something more or newer or different or better than he or she.

From all three realities, a sense of *relative deprivation* can result when comparisons are made, keeping young people in varying degrees of material dissatisfaction, suffering from the notion: "Because I don't have as much as others have, I don't have enough."

In addition, children receive another message about money as they see how the rich get treated differently than the poor. Status and social entitlement are very often associated with one's financial means. From this inequity of treatment, it is easy for children to conclude: "Wealth is worth." Coupling a sense of relative deprivation with an awareness of how money can signify personal worth, children can come to certain social conclusions as they interact with peers:

- "If I have less than, I'm not as good as."
- "If I have as much as, I'm equal to."
- "If I have more, I'm better than."

For parents, the challenge is to help the child separate monetary and material worth from self-worth.

- "If how you value yourself depends on how much money you have, then you are not placing much value on the basic human being you are."
- "If your personal happiness depends on new and more material possessions, the less your capacity for inner contentment may become."
- "If it takes having something other people want to get their attention, then that attention may not be worth very much."
- "If friends select or reject you based on what you have, then their friendship may not be worth very much."

Money and Self-Respect

Consider five sources of money a child can draw on to buy something he or she desires: *gift* money, *allowance* money, *saved* money, *earned* money, and *borrowed* money. Each source has within it some power to support self-esteem by conferring self-respect.

- *Gift money* can represent to the child that he or she is respected enough by parents to spend discretionary money in a responsible way (or else they would not allow the gift).
- *Allowance money* can represent to the child that he or she is now considered old enough to learn how to manage a regular amount of money, an allotment that may increase during adolescence to include covering some basic living expenses for which he or she becomes responsible.
- *Saved money* can represent to the child that he or she has been able to exercise sufficient self-restraint to accumulate money that otherwise could have impulsively be spent to obtain something of substantial financial cost.
- *Earned money* can represent to the child that he or she now has the power to generate independent income through holding an occasional, part-time, or regular job.
- *Borrowed money* can represent to the child that he or she can honor a loan agreement with friends or parents by paying back what is owed in a timely fashion.

Because all five sources of money can enhance self-respect, parents can support the acquisition of money when, in their judgment, it affirms self-esteem.

Setting Limits

Because parents want to be good providers for their children, wanting them to have what makes them happy, it can sometimes be hard to set limits on money for the child who may be disappointed if denied. Even worse, parents can feel that if they don't give their child enough money, or what money can buy, as others get, they are diminishing his or her self-esteem. Rather than playing into this guilt, here are some spending guidelines parents may want to consider.

1. Don't give a child more than the financial welfare of the larger family can afford.
2. Don't compete to give to your child as much as is given to your child's friends.
3. Don't blame yourselves for providing less than your child insistently wants.
4. Don't cheapen the child's self-esteem by giving in order to boost his or her self-image.
5. Don't buy for your child to compensate for actual time and attention you have not given.
6. Don't buy something to help your child manage or escape from boredom, discontent, or other unhappiness.
7. Don't give so much to the child that he or she begins to measure value to parents by the number or expense of things (toys, for example) received.
8. Don't over-give and develop unrealistic expectations of a return, and then get angry at the child for not having given back enough.

13

CREATIVITY

IMAGINATION CAN NOURISH SELF-ESTEEM

Creativity is that mental process through which people make up new and different ways of thinking and of doing things. On each creative occasion, they affirm some *interest*, increase some *capability*, and express some *individuality*. For example: a notion is conceived or a problem is solved. A game is thought up, a space is reorganized, a strategy is figured out, a formula is proposed, or a story is written. A theory is hypothesized, a poem is composed, a melody takes form, a picture is painted, a computer program is developed, an unusual business idea is proposed, or a new variation or application of something old is invented. Although society is often the ultimate beneficiary of these and many other acts of innovation, the creators themselves reap the most immediate reward: *Through the creative process, as they express their originality, they enhance their self-esteem.*

Why? Because by engaging in creative work or play, people treat themselves as a resource *worth* cultivating. They usually find the process *self*-absorbing, the expression *self*-satisfying, and the outcome *self*-affirming. Children, for example, often take obvious pride in creation: "Look at what I can do!" "Listen to what I made up!" "Let me show you a new way!" "I bet you never thought of this!"

To encourage creativity in their child, parents can both stimulate and respond to the child in powerful ways.

- They can *stimulate* the young child's imagination by playing make-believe with the boy or girl. They can read the child stories and expose the boy or girl to the wonderful world of art and invention. They can make things and make up things together by engaging in a wide variety of playful activities that begin with such opening phrases as: "Let's pretend," "Just suppose," "Picture this," "Let's see what happens when," "Let's try something different," "What if?"
- They can *respond* to the child's creation by providing an audience that affirms with their interest and appreciation what the child has made. When it's some kind of skit or skill, parental patience can be put to the test when children repeatedly want to show off their invention until they exhaust the pleasure such exposure brings: "Let me show you again!"

Because creativity is such a personal statement about one's individuality, vulnerability to disapproval and sensitivity to criticism tends to be high, particularly when it comes to the response from parents. Therefore, if parents want to nurture this powerful source of self-esteem in their child, they must do it with attention and acceptance, not disinterest and rejection.

Who Is Creative?

It is important for parents to remember that creativity is *not* some elite process reserved for a gifted few. It is for *all* children. It is there for everyone. "Original ways of seeing and responding to life are gifts every normal child brings with him [or her] in varying degrees, into the world. Many think of creativity in terms of great works of art, music, literature, or science. But we frequently overlook that creativity blossoming in small ways is just as authentic as creativity expressed in a grand manner." (see Suggested Reading,

Briggs, p. 278.) How great the creation is, is far less important, in terms of a child's self-esteem, than how good it causes the child to feel about himself or herself.

The Enemy of Creativity

Creativity can often be at the expense of *social conformity* because originality can set the individual apart from the group. In consequence, a creative difference in thinking or expression can cause a person to be treated with misunderstanding, criticism, ridicule, or even rejection for not going along with what is commonly agreed upon, widely practiced, and generally accepted.

Thus, a child may express an alternative opinion to parents and be *disapproved.* A child may question a teacher's explanation and be *punished* for challenging established authority. Or a child may show an unusual interest and be *teased* by friends for appearing "weird," which may result in *expressive inhibition.*

Expressive inhibition is very common in young children, causing them to give up certain kinds of healthy expressivity from the fear, or from the actual experience, of appearing foolish in the eyes of peers. "I can't sing." "I can't dance." "I can't draw." All of these sad conclusions are often reached after some creative expression of individuality has been socially penalized in a host of unhappy ways—by being laughed at, put down, corrected, or teased.

The more creative the child, the more nonconforming he or she may become. In the extreme, the boy or girl may be set on "marching to a different drummer" no matter what other people think. For parents, supporting the self-esteem of this determined individualist requires helping the boy or girl learn the compromise between *going with the flow* (conforming to normal demands of rules, routines, and responsibilities in life) and *going one's own way* (honoring the creative need to express one's uniqueness).

The Parent's Role

Because creativity requires exploring and expressing one's inner resources, parents can encourage the child in a number of additional ways.

- They can give time for free play, not just for organized play.
- They can expect the child to spend some time entertaining himself or herself independent of external entertainment, particularly of the passive electronic kind.
- They can be careful not to reflexively criticize or otherwise discourage a different kind of self-expression they don't understand.
- They can show interest in the child's interests when those interests do not necessarily coincide with their own.
- Within the limits of time, energy, and money they can afford, parents can support outside educational experiences through which the child can develop the creative activity that he or she loves to do.

14

COMPETENCE

LEARNING TO COPE CAN SUPPORT SELF-ESTEEM

Premature giving up is an enemy to self-esteem that tends to take two common forms: *surrender and blame.* In both cases, a child abdicates power on his or her own behalf.

Surrender

"I can't deal with that!" "This is too hard!" "It can't be fixed." "There's no point in trying." "I'll never learn!" "This is impossible!" "Why bother?" "There's nothing I can do!" Such *expressions of surrender* only create feelings of impotence. The child abandons effort in the face of frustration with what cannot be easily mastered or made right.

By refusing to attempt a difficult challenge or to influence the course of unhappy events, defeat is admitted before any struggle is begun. When a child assumes such a helpless attitude toward adversity, the role of victim is assumed, and *acting victim undercuts self-esteem.*

To the child who sees no point in trying when the likelihood of success seems small, parents can say something like this: "It's true, effort you make does not ensure the outcome that you want. However, it leaves you with the satisfaction of knowing you did all you could. And it frees you afterward from wondering if you could have made a difference if you'd only tried."

Blame

Then there are the equally disempowering *expressions of blame* through which the child casts off any responsibility for what has unhappily occurred. "It's not my fault!" "They started it." "They're the problem, not me!" "I always get treated unfairly." "Other people have all the luck!" "Why do people keep picking on me?" "If they hadn't caught me, I wouldn't be in this trouble to begin with!"

As long as the boy's or girl's entire adversity is someone else's fault, then the child has no power of choice to correct or recover from whatever has been going wrong. Only by assuming some share of responsibility for choosing his or her way into trouble, hurt, or disappointment can the child gather the decision-making power to choose his or her way out. To this child, parents can try to explain: "Instead of solving problems, blame usually makes problems worse."

Because both surrender and blame are expressions of giving up, they injure a person's self-esteem by emphasizing just how powerless one is to cope with what is going badly in one's life.

The Antidote to Giving Up

The antidote to giving up is *competence:* an approach to coping with problems in a way that enhances self-esteem. There are four components in competence that parents can support by instruction, encouragement, and example:

1. *Maintaining a can-do attitude.* "The most important step in doing what you want is believing you can do it."
2. *Assuming responsibility.* "As long as you have power of choice in life, you have power to make changes in your life."

3. *Showing persistence.* "Keep trying different approaches, and you'll keep open the possibility that you will find a way."

4. *Learning mastery.* "Keep practicing and chances are you will come to cope effectively."

What Not to Do with a Problem

One of the most powerful assumptions supporting competence is that *problems are not a problem.* Some big, but mostly small, problems are simply inevitable challenges built into everyone's daily life that occur when what people want to have happen is not what they get. Something breaks (loss). A plan is disrupted by the unexpected (surprise). There is a misunderstanding (confusion). One doesn't feel as good or look as good as one would like (disappointment). One is blocked or pushed or let down when trying to get something done (frustration). On these and many other occasions, what is the child to do?

The temptation that parents need to help the child resist is *emotional protest*, indulging feelings of displeasure at the expense of effectively coping with what has occurred. "Just look!" cries the teenager in frustration. "Just look at what I did! I can't believe it! I left out the whole middle part of the assignment and now I have to write it all over again! It's not fair! I feel like giving up and not turning in anything at all!" *In addition to wasting precious time and energy, emotional protest often encourages actions of self-defeat, thereby undercutting self-esteem.*

What parents can counsel this child is that it is okay to get upset and talk out those feelings of the moment; but it is not okay to stay upset and allow those feelings to discourage coping with the problem. *When normal problems are treated as catastrophes, emotional protest can result.*

Competence Is Being Able to Solve Problems

Whether the problem is the result of some external agent, chance circumstance, or personal miscalculation, mistake, or misdeed, parents need to encourage the child to *treat any problem as just one more opportunity to learn in life.* Their goal is not to raise a child who never does wrong and for whom nothing ever goes wrong, or to always intervene and solve the child's problems themselves. Their goal is to raise a competent child who is willing and able to figure out what to do when a problem occurs. It is rarely possible for a child to solve a problem without learning something he or she did not know before, or could not do before. *Every problem is a teacher in disguise.* And the great thing about solving a problem is that *the process comes with it's own reward*—a sense of accomplishment and pride from having successfully figured out what to do.

A simple model for helping to define a problem and sort out choices for solving it follows.

- Any problem can be defined as a statement of *dissatisfaction* over some *discrepancy* in one's life: "The way things are is not the way I want things to be." Thus, for a teenager, a problem might be this: "I am too fat!"
- To reduce this discrepancy, the problem can be solved and dissatisfaction reduced in one of two ways (or by some combination of the two).
  - The child can change the way things are to become how he or she wants them to be. The "too fat" teenager, for example, could lose weight to create the thinner appearance he or she desires.
  - Or, the child can change what he or she wants to better fit the way things are. The "too fat" teenager,

for example, could simply accept his or her husky build and come to believe such body type is okay.

Children need to be taught this problem-solving question: "*In this situation you do not like, how much can you change, and how much cannot be changed that you must come to accept?*"

With each problem solved, a measure of competence is gained, which further strengthens self-esteem. This is the larger perspective that parents can give their child: "Every time you engage with a challenge in life and do not give up or run away, you increase your ability to cope and your good feelings about yourself."

15

COMPETITION

CONTESTS CAN BUILD SELF-ESTEEM

Some children enjoy contests (tryouts, games, sports, recitals, debates, for example) and others do not. The reasons why are often rooted in contrasting attitudes toward three components of the competition itself.

1. *Conflict:* competition is an *adversary experience* in which opposition is created for recreation, winning is the objective, and losing is at stake.
2. *Cooperation:* competition is an *interdependent experience* in which collaboration with rules, with the opponent one plays, and (in the case of team sports) with other members of one's own team are all required to make the game work.
3. *Challenge:* competition is an *isometric experience* in which one gets to test the limits of one's capacities based on trying to overcome resistance the opposition provides; the harder one side plays, the harder the other must play to prevail.

The Risks of Competition

For some children, the risks of competition are more than they feel comfortable taking. What risks?

- *Exposing personal performance to comparison with others, under some degree of public scrutiny:* "Why measure myself against how someone else can do, for everyone to see?"

- *Setting oneself up for the possibility of defeat:* "Why do something where I could end up feeling bad about myself if I lose?"
- *Perhaps enduring some manner of pain*—be it emotional (from disappointment), social (from criticism), or physical (from injury): "What's the fun of maybe getting hurt?"

Then add to these risks the challenges of getting along with the adult authority in charge of preparing the child, or team of children, for competition—be it an instructor, leader, or a coach. Such a person typically acts in several capacities that some children find hard to accept.

1. *Director*—telling competitors what to do and not to do.
2. *Corrector*—telling players what was done right and wrong.
3. *Selector*—telling team members who is going to be allowed to play and when.

This combination of risk and challenge can turn off some children who prefer operating on their own terms, developing their capacities through independent or collaborative learning, or working hard at what they enjoy, by perhaps exploring and expanding themselves through some form of creative expression.

Before parents entirely foreclose on experiences of competition for this child, however, they might want to keep in mind that *the willingness to compete is a transferable skill.* After all, out in the adult world, people do compete for various kinds of opportunities like education, employment, and advancement on the job. In addition, eventually entering the workplace, they often must be able to function as a member of an organizational unit or departmental team under some "boss" authority with powers of direction, correction, and selection.

For this reason alone, it is in the interests of most children to participate in competitive activities as they grow up, joining in some kind of performance or sports team for awhile. Parents can give the child who is reluctant to participate in organized competition some measure of choice and assurance: "From a list of possibilities, you can select one to try. If, after a season, you don't like it, you can do something else."

The Rewards of Competition

Given the risks and challenges of competition, *it takes a certain amount of self-esteem to be willing* to compete. Fortunately, participation provides rewards that can make these risks and challenges feel worthwhile.

- There is *fun* from enjoyment of the event itself: "I just like being able to get out there and play."
- There is *satisfaction* from practicing skills and then putting them to the test: "I like getting better and then seeing how well I can do."
- There is a sense of *belonging* from being part of a team or group: "I like the way we all work together."
- There is *fulfillment* from trying one's hardest, win or lose: "I'm glad I gave it everything I had to give."
- There is becoming absorbed in the *intensity* of performance: "When it's just me against an opponent, I really focus on myself."
- There is *exhilaration* of defeating an opponent: "It feels great to beat the other team."

All of these rewards are powerful enhancements to self-esteem.

Unhealthy Influences from Coaches and Parents

At the same time that parents support the child's participation in some organized competition, however, they also need to monitor quality of involvement in the process for harmful influences—particularly from the child's coach or instructor, and from themselves. These influences can be damaging because each can diminish the child's self-esteem.

Competition Coaching and Instruction

There is a common style of competition coaching—*punitive coaching*—that can be quite destructive for some children who can lose enjoyment of the activity and liking for themselves in response. In this case, the coach/instructor/director is self-defined as an authority to be feared for the hurt that he or she can inflict. This person uses a variety of punitive tactics to motivate performance and maintain control.

- *Intimidation tactics* employ berating and yelling, as if to say: "If you dare play badly, you'll get worse from me!"
- *Humiliation tactics* employ sarcasm and ridicule, as if to say: "Cross me and I'll cut you down in front of others who will laugh at how I've made you look!"
- *Dissatisfaction tactics* employ criticism and blame, as if to say: "Don't get complacent, because however well you do, it's not going to be good enough!"

The more advanced the level of competition (sports in high school compared to elementary school, for example), the more the coach's employment depends on winning, the more community investment there is in winning, the more likely a child is to encounter this style of coaching some of the time.

Should this encounter occur, it's up to parents to evaluate the effect on their child's attitude toward participating in the competition, and his or her strength of self-esteem. There are some children who seem to do all right with punitive coaching, not taking it personally, treating it as one more challenge to master, even using it to strengthen their determination to play or perform.

If their child, however, is one who suffers under this kind of coaching, and if the coach is wed to this particular coaching style, parents may want to encourage the child into a different performance opportunity that is coached or instructed in a more positive way. After all, games of contest are for fun, not for punishment; to enjoy, not to endure; to enhance self-esteem, not to harm it.

A Caution to Parents

Caught up in the competition, parents themselves can be a source of harm to their child's self-esteem. Either as coach or spectator, they can become over-involved to their child's cost. They can actually engage in punitive coaching, which is usually most destructive when it come from a parent. Or as spectators, they can yell criticism of their child's play, or even loudly attack a referee for a call with which they disagree. In either case, they can be a serious embarrassment to their child, turning what was a positive experience for a child into one that feels bad.

Usually this behavior can be stopped when parents pause and remember that who they are seeing compete and perform is not some extension of themselves, but their child, who is not obliged to perform well to reflect well on them.

16

THE IMPORTANCE OF GRADES

THE EVIDENCE OF CAPACITY

Grades can be a major pillar of self-esteem when they are valued and kept in perspective, or they can be a significant detriment to self-esteem when they are not. It is up to parents to support the affirmative power of grades without allowing them to become a source of undue pressure or preoccupation for the child.

Why Grades Matter

Grades are evidence. In school, a significant arena of the child's endeavor, grades provide data on how well he or she is able to master a variety of academic tasks and skills. This feedback is evaluative, based on subjective ratings, mastery of objectives, and uniform testing by teachers. Schoolwork is a major challenge in a child's life, with grades being a measure of how adequately the child responds. They also have direct bearing on educational and occupational mobility later on.

One responsibility of parents is to establish healthy goals, standards, and limits for their child, and this includes setting appropriate expectations for school achievement. From their intimate knowledge of the child, they estimate his or her *innate capacity* (inherent talents and aptitudes), and then establish an acceptable level of *operating capacity* (actual performance) that they encourage the child to meet.

They then set a *specific floor* below which they do not want grades to go: "Believing that with a full-faith effort you could make at least all B's, we think at a minimum it's reasonable to expect you to make some mix of B's and C's." Then they promise their assistance should any grade be any less: "Get below a C, and we will do whatever we can to help you bring that grade back up." What they do *not* give are admonitions as: "Just do your best," "Just try your hardest," "Just work up to your potential." Because these abstracts do not provide measurable goals, and because no one performs up to such ideals all the time (if ever), statements such as these tend to threaten self-esteem more often than they support it. The child thinks: "How am I supposed to know how hard is hard enough?"

The power of a report card is in the feedback it can give. Parents need to help their child generate a level of performance that generally reflects his or her academic capacity, whatever level that is. By pushing the child too hard ("My parents were never happy no matter how well I did") or by pushing the child not hard enough ("My parents just didn't care how I did") parents can undermine a child's self-esteem. In the first case, the child may come to feel continually self-dissatisfied no matter how he or she excels; in the second case, the child may come to consider himself or herself not worth the effort of trying.

Keeping Grades in Perspective

To quote Louisiana psychologist Don Fontenelle: "Most parents say 'Do your best,' but don't like to see C's. Fifty percent of the children in the United States are average. The odds of having a 'C student' is greater than having an 'A-B student.' To avoid the grade issue, I urge parents to focus on responsibility and seeing the child is doing everything he or she is supposed to be doing (for example, homework, classwork, preparation for class, participation). If a child is doing everything he or she is supposed to be doing and is an A student, he or she will make A's, and if he or she is a C student, he or she will make C's." If an honest effort is made, an honest outcome will occur.

In late elementary school and junior high, it is very common in many children for this responsibility and honest effort to fall away as an *early adolescent achievement drop* occurs. Grades go down because of distraction with physical growth, social priorities with friends, and opposition to authority takeover. The most common casualty is homework, with the child "forgetting" to bring it home, lying to parents and saying there was none when there was, or grudgingly doing the homework but "forgetting" to turn it in.

In response, if reminders fail to correct the problem, parents can *supervise* the child's flagging effort

- By meeting the child at school and together making the rounds of teachers to make sure it is all brought home
- By establishing a neutral place (not the child's room) where homework will be done within a time frame, protected from interference to get it completely done
- By going up to school with the child and together making the rounds of classrooms to make sure it is all turned in

Children who faithfully do all their homework on time and turn it in, generally demonstrate what they are capable of doing at school.

Grades need to be treated as important, but their importance must not be exaggerated. For example, there are certain common parental assumptions about grades that are *not* necessarily so.

1. Good grades by the child show good parenting by the parents.
2. Children who achieve well in school will achieve well in later life.
3. High-achieving children are happy and well-adjusted, motivated and hard working, rule and law abiding, interested in learning, and mature and responsible.

The above assumptions may be true or they may be false. At a minimum, grades just go to show the teacher's evaluation of a student's work on a particular assignment, test, project, or other kind of performance averaged over a particular period of time. It is best not to read into grades much more than that, because when parents do, they risk making unrealistic assumptions that may prove costly: "But our child is an A-student, so there's no way he could be using drugs!"

Keeping Love and Approval in Perspective

Parents provide two responses to their child that have enormous value: *love* and *approval.* Through love, they convey *unconditional* acceptance of the child's *person.* Through approval, they convey *conditional* evaluation based on the child's conduct or *performance.* Love is a *given.* Approval must be *earned.* The two need to be kept separate and distinct.

Approval doesn't prove love anymore than love guarantees approval. Therefore, it can be helpful for parents to explain the difference. "Sometimes our job is unpopular, like when we say you have not acted as you should or have not performed as well as we think you could. But in neither case does our statement of disapproval have any bearing on our love for you, which will always remain as strong as ever."

Because *grades are a performance issue* they are subject to parental approval, but they should not be wed to parental acceptance. Parents who cannot honestly make this distinction often have children who believe making grades is attached to parental love. Do well and they merit that love; do badly and they risk losing it. Thus, parents who predicate their love on performance, who measure the worth of the child (and often of themselves) by his or her grades, deny their child the self-esteem that comes from securely knowing, come what may, succeed or fail, the commitment of their love is never faltering or in doubt.

The Problem of Retention

Retention is the decision to hold a child back a grade, usually for one of two reasons:

1. Because basic academic skills and performance (grades) are lacking

2. Because of physical, social, and emotional immaturity

Retention is commonly treated as giving a child a chance to re-mediate skills by repeating a year, or as being given a chance to affiliate with younger children with the same level of maturity. In either case, being held back is considered an opportunity to catch up, to do better for oneself and feel better about oneself.

Unfortunately, *research has consistently found retention to be academically counterproductive and emotionally destructive for most children of any age.* There is simply much more negative impact than positive gain.

In their article "Synthesis of Research on Grade Retention" (see *Educational Leadership*, May 1990, p. 85), authors Lorrie A. Shepard and Mary Lee Smith report: "The above research findings indicate, then, that contrary to popular belief, repeating a grade actually worsens achievement levels in subsequent years. The evidence contradicts commonsense reasoning that retention will reduce school dropout rates; it seems more likely that school policies meant to increase the number of grade retentions will exacerbate dropout rates. The negative social-emotional consequences of repeating represents the only area where conventional wisdom is consistent with research findings: kids have always hated being retained, and the studies bear that out."

Many of these children will describe themselves as "losers," as "repeaters," and as being "stupid," too stupid to learn, so they give up trying. *For children of any age, retention is risky because it can have an enormous de-motivating effect.* They have literally failed to make the grade. The obvious alternative, however, *social promotion*, has its own set of woes. The child is advanced to meet an even more difficult set of academic demands than those he or she failed to master before.

So what is the best answer? Probably a compromise between social promotion and *supplemental education*—the socially promoted child is given additional academic assistance to catch up and keep up with the new set of educational demands.

17

THE POWER OF PEERS

THE IMPACT OF SOCIAL CRUELTY

To varying degrees, around grades three through six, student treatment of classmates can be very hard on children's self-esteem. Why? Because as girls and boys begin the separation from childhood into early adolescence (typically between the ages of 9 and 13), a host of developmental changes begin to revolutionize and destabilize their lives. Mostly out of their control and against their wills—physically, emotionally, sexually, and socially—they start to become different from how they used to be, and were used to being, as a child. *Growing up requires giving up old identity as the price of admission into adolescence that every child must pay.*

In this inevitable process, the two components of self-esteem are significantly impacted. *Self-definition* is now in question because of all the new, uncertain changes going on. And *self-evaluation* becomes harsher as self-consciousness and insecurity from feeling different cause children to unfavorably compare themselves with others. In consequence, feelings of inadequacy and doubt can be created. Anxiety, loss of confidence, and low self-esteem that are endemic to the age now infect peer relationships to almost everyone's cost.

The rules of social treatment and social friendship dramatically alter—mostly for the worse. Holding or advancing one's social position in the class becomes a primary means of compensating for universal feelings of personal deficiency every child believes are unique to him or her. Claiming as much popularity as possible (by being nice to popular people) and avoiding as much unpopularity as possible (by being mean to unpopular people) become common goals.

How Social Cruelty Works

In classrooms, on the bus, in the halls, in the lunchroom, and on the playground, *ganging-up behavior* may become more common, as *followers* follow the lead of a *bully* (who is socially dominant) in tormenting a *victim* (who often possesses some unfortunate difference), so they do not become victimized themselves. *Intimidation* (pushing, threatening, vandalizing), *exclusion* (ignoring, rejecting, casting out), *embarrassment* (nicknaming, teasing, cutting down), and the *attacking of reputation* (rumor, gossip, slander) can all come into play in seriously harmful ways for all parties concerned.

Spending time in any of the three social cruelty roles—bully, follower, or victim—has the potential of injuring self-esteem. Although the bully gains social dominance by abusing social power, he or she has more allies of the moment than actual friends. To be feared is not the same as being liked. Although the follower escapes mistreatment by joining in, he or she must contend with feelings of cowardice. To go along to keep from getting hurt is to sacrifice some self-respect. Although the victim is the beneficiary of social attention, it is of a hurtful and sometimes scary kind. To be continually targeted for mistreatment is to run the risk of coming to believe it is deserved.

Possible long-term learnings from these three roles are important for parents to consider.

- *To remain a bully* may lead the child into engaging in coercion at the expense of intimacy as an adult.

- *To remain a follower* may lead the child into subscribing to obedience at the expense of integrity as an adult.
- *To remain a victim* may lead the child to suffer from helplessness at the expense of competence as an adult.

"Now is later," because present behavior shapes future conduct. When parents influence how the child develops, they affect how the adult becomes.

For parents, the lesson is simply this: If you ever have cause to believe your child is consistently acting in any of the three social cruelty roles at school or in the neighborhood, talk to him or her about the costs and the choices, because every child has some choice in defining the role he or she plays.

What to Do When Your Child Becomes a Victim of Social Cruelty

But what should parents do, usually feeling victimized themselves, if their child is regularly cast in the role of social victim at school? There are some helpful actions to take.

1. Listen to feelings and let the child know there is no shame in feeling hurt or fear.
2. Help analyze the situations to make sure that the child is not making a bad situation worse by unwittingly acting to attract or reward mistreatment.
3. Support the social courage it takes to face social cruelty at school each day because bravery now may strengthen the child for other challenges later on.
4. Help the child understand that as long as he or she keeps trying new and different ways of coping, power of active choice can diminish passive feelings of being a victim, and can support sense of self-control and self-esteem.

5. Help the child understand that avoidance and running away may increase his or her fear and encourage the tormentors.

6. Help the child not fall into the trap of being a loner, but initiate friendship with other students in the class who never participate in the bully or follower roles.

7. Provide perspective by explaining how this mistreatment has to do with the age, not any deficiency in the child's person, and how the need for social cruelty subsides as children grow older and become more secure.

8. Permit the child to take a more socially aggressive role (practice standing up to and fighting back) against this treatment if persistently ignoring social cruelty has failed to diminish its occurrence or make it go away.

9. Make sure that the child takes appropriate responsibility: *There is no such thing as a self-made bully.* A bully is made when people give that person permission to push them around.

10. Enroll the child in other social circles outside of school and support the child having new friends over to play.

11. If incidents of social cruelty are occurring within the classroom, with the child's permission, ask the teacher to intervene, letting all students know the safe and respectful standards of treatment and communication that are expected to be followed there.

12. If despite all attempts by the child, support from the parents, and appeals to the school, mistreatment

continues and the boy's or girl's self-esteem is being severely damaged, get outside counseling help to prevent severe social cruelty from having a long-term, damaging psychological effect. Trouble signs to look for can include becoming despondent, withdrawn, socially isolated, or self-depreciating.

Finally, if, despite talking with the teacher, continuing acts of social cruelty reach a level where fears for the child's emotional, physical, or sexual safety appear justified, parents should appeal to higher powers within the school or school system to put a stop to the mistreatment and the damage being done.

18

ADD (ATTENTION DEFICIT DISORDER)

WHEN ATTENDING AND COMPLYING ARE HARD TO DO

There is a condition that adversely affects the self-esteem of increasing numbers of children in our country today, one that is extremely challenging to help. The diagnostic label ADD (Attention Deficit Disorder) has been given more frequently in recent years to describe a constellation of behaviors first noticed at home but often not formally identified until teachers express concerns about the child's conduct at school.

These highly distractible children seem to be "wired" with such a high need for stimulation that they labor under two kinds of *deficits*. They find it *difficult to concentrate sustained attention* on instruction, and find it *frustrating not to get all the attention they want*. In consequence, they are often *governed by a level of impulsiveness* that makes concentrating on tasks and complying with social limits very hard to do.

These high-energy boys and girls are often in trouble with the powers that be in the family and in the classroom. They frequently get treated with impatience, disapproval, criticism, reprimand, and punishment for not staying on task, not completing assignments, not listening, not following directions, not complying with a request, not getting organized, not remembering, not sitting still, not keeping quiet, not awaiting a turn, not achieving up to capacity, and not readily doing what they are told.

Adult Response to ADD Can Injure Self-Esteem

How children are treated influences how they learn to treat themselves. Reactions to them can be interpreted as reflections of them: "How other people see me must be how I am." Because of this connection, the increased incidence of negative responses by significant adults can cause ADD children to become unduly critical of themselves. *Self-rejecting, they can blame themselves with pejorative labels that do their self-esteem no good*—"the misfit," "the weirdo," "the discipline problem," "the troublemaker," "the dumb kid," "the bad kid," "the failure."

Parents who see the ADD child making this self-critical connection and putting on any of these labels need to explain that ADD is a functional condition, not a personal flaw. As they would about any functional condition, parents need to assure the child:

1. That he or she is *not* at fault for his or her constitutional state
2. That his or her human worth or value is no way diminished by this condition
3. That there is a need to understand how this condition affects his or her mental functioning in order to develop strategies for managing it

What Little Is Known About ADD

Although there may be physiological sources of ADD behavior (brain injury, prenatal toxic exposure, genetic abnormalities, for example), in very many cases no such factors can be found. As concluded by a 1998 National Institutes of Health panel (*Science News*, vol. 154, p. 343), exactly what causes ADD, how to precisely diagnose it, and how best to treat it are all questions that need much more scientific work before significant consensus and precise understanding can be reached.

What seems likely, however, is the following:

- Perhaps as many as two million children between the ages of 5 and 14 are ADD affected, with the incidence appearing to grow.
- Although boys and girls are both susceptible, boys are diagnosed five to ten times more frequently, probably because they tend to act out symptoms in more socially aggressive ways.
- In some cases, psycho-stimulant medication seems to help reduce impulsiveness and distractibility, the chemical perhaps increasing needed brain stimulation, thus settling the child's behavior down (although the long-term effects of this treatment on learning, development, and the nervous system are yet to be determined).
- As a population, ADD children may be at statistically higher risks than the general population for family problems, school failure, alcohol and drug abuse, criminal behavior, accidents of all sorts, and suicide.
- "Children with attention deficit disorder generally don't outgrow their difficulties. Problems that emerge or persist in adolescence and adulthood include academic failure, *low self-esteem* [italics mine], anxiety, depression, and difficulty in learning appropriate social behavior." (See Suggested Reading, Merck, p. 1253.)

An Additional Explanation: Stimulus Overload Adjustment (SOA)

Considering the cultural conditioning they receive, it is possible that a significant number of children diagnosed ADD are mislabeled. For many of these children, a better term might be *Stimulus Overload Adjustment* (*SOA*). SOA could be *a conditioned response to growing up in an over-stimulating technological world* that can cause children to learn to need, even to depend on, a constant diet of quickly changing, passively received, high-sensation stimuli to feel okay. Anything less, like formal education, can feel like cruel and unusual punishment, a kind of sensory stimuli deprivation that some children experience as intolerably boring, hence the frequency of ADD-like behaviors disrupting the classroom today.

Given all the electronic recreational choices at their command, it is little wonder that:

- Children expect to be entertained more and can independently entertain themselves less
- Attention span is diminishing as electronic choices increase
- Demand for variety in stimulation is growing
- It takes more powerful stimuli to hold their interest
- Boredom is increasingly harder to tolerate

The passive, exciting, entertainment training provided by our culture ill prepares many of our children for the dull, active, educational demands encountered in the classroom. *Most classroom education cannot compete with the culture of entertainment when it comes to attracting and holding a child's attention.*

The Counter-Cultural Prescription

So what are parents (and teachers) to do with more and more high-stimulus dependent children appearing on the scene? As mentioned at the outset, a predominantly negative adult response only injures the child's self-esteem, no matter how defiantly the child proclaims not to care. *What is needed with these children is direction, not correction.*

Parents can try to counter the high entertainment, high-stimulation influence of our culture by helping the child *practice* and develop self-management skills in the family that may tend to reduce the incidence of unproductive behaviors both there and at school. Here are a few suggestions.

- Help the child learn to quietly relax independently of external distraction.
- Limit passive electronic entertainment so the child also does active recreation.
- Help the child learn to delay gratification, tolerate frustration, and talk out (as opposed to act out) emotional upset.
- Make sure to acknowledge and approve such common behaviors as listening, following directions, remembering, completing an unenjoyable task, keeping a commitment, working to achieve a goal, attending to details, keeping personal space and belongings organized, and doing a job on time.
- Insist that the child has regular, *boring* household chores to accomplish, and express appreciation when a chore is done.
- Coach the child in anticipatory thinking—slowing down decision making by considering possible consequences for actions to be taken.

Parents who take the supervisory time to teach their child effective self-management may reduce the tyranny of impulse and stimulation over these children's lives. *By gaining a greater sense of self-control, these children recover injured self-esteem.*

What About Medication?

Many children for whom the ADD diagnosis is made find psycho-stimulant medication to be extremely helpful. There is the downside of psycho-stimulant medication, however, in addition to such possible adverse side effects as headaches, stomachaches, insomnia, or depression. There is this larger problem: *the increasingly common use of such medication with children not for purposes of improved self-management, but for ease of institutional social control.* An ADD evaluation may be recommended in hopes that medication will be prescribed "to settle the student down." Because medicated children become more socially manageable children, however, is no good reason to place them on such a chemical regimen.

If parents are advised to pursue an ADD evaluation of their child, but want to reduce the likelihood of misdiagnosis, they may want to get a second, independent opinion if a first positive identification is made. And because of the complexities connected with this condition, they should get themselves educated about the problem. Two good sources are:

1. The National Association for Children with Attention Deficit Disorder (CHADD) (1-800-233-4050)
2. *Keys To Parenting a Child with Attention Deficit Disorder* (see Suggested Reading)

19

THE HARD HALF OF GROWING UP

PITFALLS ON THE WAY TO INDEPENDENCE

A*dolescence* begins around the onset of puberty (ages nine to thirteen), when the boy or girl starts contesting old restraints and demanding new freedoms. It ends about 10 to 12 years later, when the young man or woman has now learned enough responsibility to undertake living on more self-supporting terms (ages eighteen to twenty-three).

This transition from dependency as a child to independence as a young adult does *not* happen overnight. It is a long and challenging journey through many changes—through ups and downs, success and failure, two steps forward and one step back—a halting progress that can fill parents with hopes one moment and frustration the next.

What can help parents keep their balance through the unsteady teenage years is to be able to anticipate some of the normal changes the young person is growing through, and particularly to be on the watch for certain *developmental pitfalls* along the way.

How Adolescence Can Be Dangerous to Self-Esteem

At each of the four stages of adolescence, a young person, may cope with the challenges of growth by engaging in self-defeating behaviors that can injure self-esteem. It is up to parents to be aware of these self-defeating behaviors and to counter any of them should they occur.

Stage One: Early Adolescence (Ages Nine to Thirteen)

Early adolescence begins the separation from childhood. The young person, now dissatisfied with being defined and being treated as just a child, wants something older and different, unsure precisely what. Often restless and easily frustrated at this time, the boy or girl typically

- Displays a more *negative attitude* (is critical of others and complains about life)
- Becomes more *actively and passively resistant* (is argumentative and delays compliance)
- Begins early *experimentation with the forbidden* (tests rules and limits to see what can be gotten away with)

At this stage, *the young person is at risk of rebelling against self-interest for opposition's sake.* A common example of this danger is acting out disruptively in class. In words and actions, the young person, on principle of self-determination, resists complying with rules: "Why should I have to do what I'm told when it's not what I want?" Unfortunately, such *defiance is self-defeating because it invites consequences (being sent to the office) that interfere with learning.* Grades, a major pillar of self-esteem, begin to suffer. Proudly but sadly the young person admits: "What I'm best at is getting in trouble."

In response to their child's rebellious choice, parents can make an invasive, and possibly embarrassing, response. "If you can't assume responsibility for not acting out during instruction, I am willing to come up to school and sit beside you to help you take care of business in class."

Stage Two: Mid-Adolescence (Ages Thirteen to Sixteen)

In mid-adolescence, the young person complains less about the unfairness of parents determining his or her personal freedom, and contests more strongly their capacity to do so. At stake in the increased frequency and intensity of conflict that results is the gaining of more worldly experience for growth, as the teenager objects more to restraints and argues for more independence. What is commonly the most stormy period of the adolescent passage has begun.

At this stage, *a young person is at risk of resorting to evasive behavior to get social freedom that is desired.* A common example of this danger is *mid-adolescent lying.* By omission and commission, teenagers lie to get to do what has been forbidden and to escape consequences of getting caught.

Buying freedom with deceit, however, is like borrowing freedom now for trouble later. In more cases than not, the rewards are not worth the price because the costs of lying can be so high. Psychologically, *lying is self-defeating behavior of a very serious kind because it does enormous damage to self-esteem.* Consider just a few of the injuries that are sustained. Liars lack the confidence and courage to face up to what is really going on. Liars act increasingly fugitive, driven by the fear of being found out. Liars allow dishonesty to create distance and distrust between themselves and those they love. Liars tell one lie to cover up another, can't keep all their stories straight, and end up feeling out of control.

To counter lying, parents must keep taking healthy stands for truth. Therefore, every time they catch the young person in a lie, they confront the teenager with how it feels to be lied to. They give the teenager an opportunity to confess the truth. They discuss how lying has changed for the worse how parents and teenager live together. They assess consequences—short-term grounding or an extra job to work off the serious offense of lying. And they reinstate trust so the teenager has another opportunity to live with them on truthful terms.

Stage Three: Late Adolescence (Ages Sixteen to Eighteen)

By late adolescence, the grievance and negativity of early adolescence and the intense conflict and endless evasion of mid-adolescence have usually subsided. Now, true independence is in sight. No longer just a romantic dream for the teenager, it has now become a sobering reality. Seen by the young person for what it actually is, independence represents more separation from family, more acceptance of responsibility, and more expectation of self-support. When the late adolescent really thinks about it, *real independence is really scary.*

At this stage, a young person is at risk of having second thoughts about independence, deciding to retreat from this challenge instead of accepting it and moving on. A common example is *next-step reluctance.* Fearful of letting go of so much that is secure and familiar, and of facing so much that is untried and unknown, the late adolescent may delay departure by delaying preparations for what comes next.

This delay goes beyond mere procrastination because it is not based on putting off the undesirable, but on running away from the inevitable. Thus, job or educational applications languish from inattention as the high school senior tries to pretend and play like there is no tomorrow. However, a serious price is paid: *Resisting progress is self-defeating because avoiding growing up lowers self-esteem.* At a time when the older teenager wants to be filled with eagerness and hope, he or she is acting crippled by dread instead.

At this juncture, there is a role for parental support. To help their son or daughter overcome next-step reluctance, they brave one final battle for their child's good by reminding, nagging, pushing, even helping the young person accomplish the paper or interview preparation that is required for moving on. Leaving home not fully ready for independence is not a problem; it is to be expected. Parents can only prepare their child so much. Then they must turn their son or daughter over to the big **R**, *Reality*, to teach the rest.

Stage Four: Trial Independence (Ages Eighteen to Twenty-three)

In trial independence, the young person begins trying to live on his or her own and usually finds the challenge more difficult than anticipated. Because there are so many commitments that must be kept if independence is to be successfully maintained, most young people cannot manage to meet all these responsibilities, all the time, right away. Slipping and sliding as they struggle to find a stable footing, they typically break a certain number of significant commitments—from personal promises to bill obligations, to credit arrangements, to rental agreements, to local statutes, to job requirements, and to educational standards, to name a few.

Making matters worse are two influences that can destabilize young people even further. First, they are surrounded by a cohort of similarly unsteady friends who are often inclined to procrastinate, play, and party at the expense of taking care of business, sometimes acting as wild as full freedom will allow. And second, the three to five years after high school tend to be the most alcohol and drug intensive period they have ever seen or experienced.

At this stage, *the young person is at risk of indulging in freedom at the expense of responsibility*. A common example of this is *credit card debt*. Treating "plastic as permission," young people may blithely charge to enjoy what they cannot afford, only to be brought up short by a threatening creditor finally demanding to be paid or else.

To cope, a young person may appeal to parents to borrow money or to be bailed out, promising not to ever need such assistance again. *Asking to be rescued from the consequences of one's own unwise choices is self-defeating because refusing to take responsibility for recovery lowers self-esteem.*

In response, strong parents may decide to give the hardest help of all: the refusal to help. In doing so, they communicate that they respect the young person enough to believe that he or she has what it takes to work off the debt that impulsive spending has created, and to learn more self-discipline and self-sufficiency in the process.

The purpose of all these parental interventions during the different stages of adolescence is the same: to encourage a healthy alternative to common self-defeating behaviors through which young people can injure their self-esteem. Key to the effectiveness of each intervention is a missing ingredient in all four: *Criticism plays no part in what the parents say or do.*

20

MALE AND FEMALE

SEX ROLE DEFINITIONS MAKE A DIFFERENCE

A child's *sex* is biologically determined; a child's *sex role* is not. *Sex role is learned.* A boy or girl primarily learns how to act "male" or "female" based on *parental, peer,* and *media* influences that he or she has known.

Parents

Deeply rooted in years of attachment, imprinted through endless daily interactions, parental influences are usually implied and not declared, taken for granted and not discussed, thus, hard for parents and child to see. Hindsight, when one becomes a young adult, is often required to bring these influences into focus at last.

- Looking back, the young person notices similarities to each parent that suggest some degree of *parental identification* (with a parental interest, for example).
- The young man or woman may also notice that there were different kinds of *parental treatment* based on the sex of the child (around social freedom, for example).
- The young person may recall different *parental expectations* depending on the child's sex (toward education, for example).

All three influences are part of the parental effect on a child's sex role development.

If parents want to be more intentional about their sex role influence from the start, they can take stock of their sex role preconceptions by completing the following statements:

"Boys should be..." (add adjectives)
"Boys should *not* be..." (add adjectives)

"Boys should..."(add action words)
"Boys should *not* ..." (add action words)

"Girls should be..." (add adjectives)
"Girls should *not* be..." (add adjectives)

"Girls should ..."(add action words)
"Girls should *not*..." (add action words)

What this inventory yields are parental sex role beliefs and values, how those beliefs and values differ for male and female children, and where parents agree and disagree. Most important, it clarifies approved and disapproved definitions that can be checked to see if they are actually compatible with the inborn nature (personality, temperament, intelligence) of their child.

To force a child into a sex role definition that simply does not fit (for example, a boy who doesn't like killing to love hunting like his father; a girl who prefers having a few close friends to wanting extreme popularity like her mother) can be extremely hurtful to a child's self-esteem. Falling short of the mark, the child may end up feeling inadequate for being different, a disappointment, a failure, or otherwise diminished because he or she does not meet the sex role modeled or desired by the parent.

In general, *it helps if parents keep the broadest possible view of sex role definition in mind by remembering that there are as many ways of being female as there are women alive, and there as many ways of being male as there are men alive. What matters for each child is arriving at a sex role definition that works as happily and healthily as possible for that individual boy or girl.*

Peers

Through early adolescence (about ages nine to thirteen), most socializing is done in same-sex peer groups—boys primarily enjoying the company of boys and girls primarily enjoying the company of girls. Life in these same-sex peer groups has enormous formative effect on sex role development as members learn to *conform* to the norms of their own group and learn from their fellows how the other sex supposedly *contrasts* to them.

The results of this early socialization are very powerful. By junior high or middle school, the lines delineating sex role differences have often been very clearly drawn, dividing the full spectrum of human traits in two—one set considered appropriate for males, another set considered appropriate for females. For example, the list of different traits might look like this. *Males are usually more*: tough, daring, confrontational, aggressive, challenging, and competitive. *Females are usually more*: sensitive, caring, supportive, responsive, confiding, and collaborative.

The sad thing about such arbitrary sex role differences is how dehumanizing they can be, limiting a young person to certain sex approved traits, and prohibiting or even punishing the expression of others. Thus, a boy who manifests "female" traits listed above may seem *unmanly* in the eyes of both male and female peers, whereas a girl may seem *unwomanly* to male and female peers when she manifests traits considered more appropriate for "males."

For example, if the sex role expectation is that males can get angry but not show pain, and females can show pain but not get angry, then a boy who cries may be called a "wimp," and a girl who loses her temper may be called a "witch." To make matters worse, in order to protect themselves from terms so damaging to reputation and hence self-esteem, boys may learn to cover up their pain by masking it as anger (cursing), whereas girls may learn to cover up their anger by masking it as pain (crying).

Although parents cannot conduct their child's friendships, or participate in daily interactions that go on at school, they can treat their son or daughter as a "whole person" at home, for example, encouraging the "sensitive" side of their manly son who wants to be emotionally supportive and the "daring" side of their womanly daughter who wants to be adventurous.

Finally, parents should be aware of some *traditional* sex role definitions that still have some bearing on how male and female children can be socialized differently to develop their self-esteem. Boys often tend to define their worth primarily based on how they *perform,* doing well (achieving) as a major pillar of self-esteem. Girls often tend to define their worth primarily based on how they *relate,* being liked (socially connecting) as a major pillar of self-esteem. Thus, when a good friend ends a friendship or moves away, a girl may be more likely to feel seriously injured than a boy; but when a boy doesn't make, or is dropped from, a team, he may be more likely to feel seriously injured than a girl.

Due to the degree that traditional differences shape and limit sex role development, parents may want to support *both* the performing and relating sources of self-esteem in their child. When each is in place, a girl who is feeling down on herself because relationships are going badly has avenues of performing well that can buoy her up during a hard time. And a boy who is feeling down on himself for performing badly can have close friendships that hold him in good stead when efforts to achieve have not gone well.

Media

The media—advertising and popular entertainment—use *social stereotypes* and *physical ideals* with impressionable young people to attract their attention, shape their tastes, and get their business, striving to turn *human beings* into consumers (*human buyers*) at the earliest possible age. In addition to being commercially exploitive, these images can also be unhealthy. Such stereotypes and ideals can be destructive in two ways.

- By being oversimplified and extreme, they are unrealistic in the human definition they promote.
- By pushing perfection, they present a standard that young people, no matter how desperately they try, will fail to meet.

Unhappily, at least for the young consumers, these commercial images have enormous motivational effect. Because they are so glamorized, they shape much of the self-definition that young people seek. One stereotypical male ideal, for example, is *the action hero tough guy*, an image that can encourage boys, even in elementary school, to start muscling up and to act more aggressive. One stereotypical female ideal is *the ultra-thin beautiful model*, an image that can encourage girls, also from an early age, to diet down in order to be attractive.

In striving to fit these stereotypes and ideals in order to enhance self-esteem, young people can actually do themselves significant harm. In order to meet the tough/aggressive ideal, boys at school can challenge authority, resist rules, and get in fights. Perhaps this partly explains why a disproportionate number of males, as opposed to females, receive disciplinary referrals, get suspended, and drop out of school, threatening their future well-being. In order to meet the thin/attractive ideal, girls can diet and starve or binge and purge. Perhaps this partly explains why a disproportionate number of females, as opposed to males, are prone to eating disorders, which threaten their health and in some cases their lives.

Parents must editorialize to their children about social stereotypes and physical ideals being offered by the media, pointing out how these images provide unworkable and unhealthy models for developing one's sex role definition. They can explain how:

- *Ideals are fantasy*, not reality.
- *Stereotypes oversimplify*, they are not accurate.
- *Perfection only provides an inhuman standard that people are not meant to meet.*

21

HETEROSEXUAL OR HOMOSEXUAL

ORIENTATION MAKES A DIFFERENCE

The impact of sexual orientation is less on the side of self-definition, the first component of self-esteem, than on the second, *self-evaluation*. Heterosexual young people (sexually attracted to members of the opposite sex) take for granted feeling comfortable and secure in their sexual orientation because the majority of social and cultural norms treat this orientation as the way most people are "meant" to be. Homosexual young people (sexually attracted to members of their own sex), however, are not granted this luxury of social acceptance. Because they depart from the "norm," they are subject to social attitudes and treatment of a rejecting kind that can cause a gay boy or girl to be rejecting of himself or herself, inflicting deep injury to self-esteem.

- Experiencing *anti-gay prejudice*, insult, and humor, the young person can feel personally devalued.
- Experiencing *anti-gay discrimination*, the young person can feel personally shunned, denied, and excluded.
- Experiencing *anti-gay violence*, the young person can feel personally threatened, or be actually harmed, by verbal and physical attack.

No wonder so many young people go into deep hiding about their homosexual orientation. Fearing discovery, they seek safety in concealment, paying two personal costs extremely damaging to self-esteem—loneliness from an isolating sense of being different and self-criticism or at least self-doubt from not meeting the dominant heterosexual expectation.

"Homosexual kids must wrestle not only with the usual identity crises and struggles for independence common to all teenagers, but also with society's stigmatization of anyone who is not heterosexual. So at the same time these youngsters are beginning to feel attracted to individuals of the same sex, they are hearing about and witnessing homophobia in all its many forms, from unkind stereotyping of and jokes about homosexuals on TV sitcoms to unprovoked, violent attacks on gay men and women in real life." (See Suggested Reading, Fassler and Dumas, p. 108.)

Current Medical Thought About Homosexuality

Not only do parents need to be sensitive to the special challenges to self-esteem that being homosexual can pose for their child, they also need to get their heads straight about the nature and occurrence of homosexuality itself.

"...*Homosexuality*, once considered abnormal by the medical profession, is no longer considered a disorder; it is widely recognized as a sexual orientation that is present from childhood. The prevalence of homosexuality is unknown, but it is estimated that about 6 to 10 percent of adults are involved exclusively in homosexual relationships throughout their lives. A much higher percentage of people have experimented with same-sex activities in adolescence but are heterosexually orientated as adults.

"The causes of homosexuality aren't known, nor are the causes of heterosexuality. No particular hormonal, biologic, or psychologic influences have been identified as substantially contributing to a person's sexual orientation. Homosexuals discover they are attracted to people of the same sex, just as heterosexuals discover they are attracted to people of the opposite sex. The attraction appears to be the end result of biologic and environmental influences and isn't a matter of deliberate choice. Therefore, the popular term 'sexual preference' makes little sense in matters of sexual orientation.

"Most homosexuals adjust well to their sexual orientation, although they must overcome widespread societal disapproval and prejudice. That adjustment may take a long time and may be associated with substantial psychologic stress. Many homosexual men and women experience bigotry in social situations and in the workplace, adding to their stress." (See Suggested Reading, Merck, pp. 417–418.)

What Surveys Report About Homosexuality

Homosexual young people in this country grow up in a world of profoundly anti-gay sentiment and behavior, both of which make feeling good about oneself and feeling socially safe very difficult, particularly in the world of school.

- According to "a nationwide poll of 13-to-17-year-olds conducted by the *New York Times* and CBS News…58 percent of boys and 47 percent of girls say homosexuality is 'always wrong.'" (*New York Times*, 30 April 1998; p. A1.)
- "Last year, in a survey of almost 4,000 Massachusetts high school students, 22 percent of gay respondents said they had skipped school in the last month because they felt unsafe there, and 31 percent said they had been threatened or injured in the past year. These percentages were about five times greater than the percentages of heterosexual respondents. The survey was conducted at 58 high schools by the Massachusetts Department of Education." (*New York Times*, 14 October 1998; p. A17.)

If parents have been informed by their child that he or she is gay, they must have open communication with their son or daughter about the impact of anti-gay jokes, insults, threats, and actions to which he or she may have been witness or object, particularly at school. The child may need help not taking anti-gay sentiment personally: "It's about something wrong with them, not about anything wrong with you." And intervention may be required to protect against mistreatment just as one would against anti-racial or anti-religious attacks against one's child. *Parents who understand, accept, and stand up for their gay child do much to support his or her self-esteem.*

Depression and Suicide

Being a gay young person does not simply increase the risk of violence from *homophobic* others whose *fear of homosexuality* can translate into hate-filled verbal or physical attacks; being gay also increases the risk of violence to oneself. "These (gay) kids don't want to be feared and disliked, and they certainly don't want to lose the respect and love of friends and relatives. But they often find it difficult to suppress their sexual needs and desires. When homosexual and bisexual children feel ashamed, confused, different, and socially isolated, it's hard for them to develop the kind of self-esteem and resiliency they need to defend themselves against the emotional problems, particularly depression, that increase their risk for suicide." (See Suggested Reading, Fassler and Dumas, p. 108.)

"The suicide rate for gay teens is particularly distressing... According to one recent study, gay youths account for up to *30 percent* of all teenage suicides. And in another study of gay and bisexual males, nearly *one third* of them reported that they had attempted suicide at least once... These problems are caused not by homosexuality but rather by society's *misunderstanding* of homosexuality... Homophobia—not homosexuality itself—is what makes the lives of gay people so difficult... The most helpful thing we can do is to teach...that homosexuality is nothing to fear and nothing to hate." (See Suggested Reading, Pollack, pp. 209–210.) One way to discourage homophobic attitudes in children at home is to explain the harm done by anti-gay humor and anti-gay slurs (just as one would the harm done by racial or religious insults) and prohibit their use in family communication.

What Can Parents Do When Their Child "Comes Out?"

This Key has relied primarily on experts in the field for the advice to parents being offered. In closing, one reliable source responds to the question of what parents can do when their child discloses to them that he or she is gay. There is this advice from The American Academy of Pediatrics: "Your own child's sexual orientation is actually established quite firmly by the middle years. But since there is little opportunity to test and act out this orientation, it may not be evident to the family until adolescence or even later... Sexual orientation cannot be changed. A child's heterosexuality or homosexuality is deeply ingrained as part of them. You need to be supportive and helpful, no matter what your youngster's sexual orientation may be." (See Suggested Reading, Schor, pp. 138–139.)

22

SOCIAL OPPRESSION

WHEN MINORITY STATUS IS DISADVANTAGED

According to the American Academy of Pediatrics: "Children can suffer from a climate of prejudice. Prejudice creates social and emotional tension and can lead to fear and anxiety and occasionally to hostility and violence. Prejudice and discrimination can undermine the self-esteem and self-confidence of those being ridiculed and make them feel terrible, unaccepted, and unworthy." (See Suggested Reading, Schor, p. 162.) Consider just a few examples of the injury that can be done.

- A mentally retarded child is mimicked on the playground and laughed at for being "slow."
- An early maturing young woman is exposed to sexual taunts and molestation from young men as she passes down the hall between classes.
- Year after year, students of a particular racial group continue to be disproportionately underrepresented in schoolwide organizations.
- Inside his locker, a boy finds an anonymous hate message attacking him for his religious beliefs and warning him to watch out.
- A student is socially excluded from an extracurricular activity because the family cannot afford special expenses required for travel, dress, or equipment to belong.

- Students who are native to the community expect, and receive, preferential instructional placement at school over immigrant students who are considered less capable because they lack fluency in English.
- A teacher uses negative stereotypes when describing "those people" in a class where members of the offended group are in attendance.
- A boy or girl, given a nickname to ridicule his or her heavy weight is also socially shunned, continually selected last when other students are picked for teams.

For many children, mistreatment based on being *different* from the ruling social majority is first painfully experienced at school, and when it occurs, a parent usually feels victimized as well. What individual differences can be subject to social mistreatment? Unfortunately, there are a host of kinds, having to do with such basic characteristics as personal appearance, mental functioning, physical functioning, economic background, sex, sexual orientation, primary language, ethnicity, race, and religious beliefs, to name a few.

To see one's children criticized, excluded, threatened, or pushed around for being different from the majority at school only suggests to a parent what may be in store for them growing up with some kind of minority status in a larger society

- Whose dominant norms may be biased against accepting them
- Whose freedom of opportunity may be limited by unequal access
- Whose security may be diminished by less public protection

Social oppression is what happens when a majority in any

social system acts to keep "different" or minority individuals at a disadvantage—down, and out, and unsafe. ("Majority" is not necessarily determined by superior numbers, but politically by dominant social influence and economic power.)

Effects of Social Oppression on Self-Esteem

There are *three agents of social oppression*, and each can severely injure self-esteem.

1. Expressions of *prejudice*, usually in the form of negative stereotypes, communicate to the victim that his or her "kind" is inferior, thereby attacking that person's self-evaluation, one component of self-esteem. Prejudice is learned by generalizing from an individual *negative contact* (cheated by one person, the target decides to distrust all members of the group to which that person belongs) or by *hearsay* (told by a trusted one of "us" what "they" are all like, a prejudiced informant is believed). *The power of prejudice is the poison of self-rejection:* victims coming to believe the social judgment made against them. Thus, gay young people must usually struggle to accept their homosexuality because of what the majority heterosexual culture has taught them to believe. Years of witnessing anti-gay beliefs, jokes, and attacks in the larger society and at school have encouraged them to learn prejudice against themselves.

2. Acts of *discrimination*, usually in the form of obstruction or exclusion, keep the victim from developing to full potential, thereby limiting one's self-definition, the other component of a person's self-esteem. The more against the law discrimination has been declared, the less overt and more covert it has become (other "reasons" to deny a meritorious

person opportunity are found). *The power of discrimination is the denial of opportunity*: victims coming to be restricted by what they are not allowed to do. Thus, students entering high school with limited English-speaking ability may be tracked into all low-level courses, with lack of fluency in the majority language used to limit everything they are allowed to learn.

3. Acts of *harassment*, usually in the form of threats or attack, communicate to the victim a sense of personal danger, distracting a young person at school from learning in the interests of preserving safety, thereby undermining self-esteem by sacrificing academic performance. The frightening influence of a single example can be profound ("If that could happen to one of us, it could happen to all of us"). *The power of harassment is intimidation*, causing victims to live on such fearful terms that they often dare not confront what they know is wrong. Thus, young women who are subject to unwelcome male sexual advances at school—sexual comments, sexual name-calling, sexual pressure, sexual gestures, sexual touch, or sexual molestation—"report effects similar to those of rape victims—anger, fear, powerlessness, shame and self-blame, loss of self-esteem, guilt, confusion, depression, embarrassment." (*Vocational Education Journal*, March 1993, p. 30.) "The American Association of University Women...reports that 70 percent of girls experience harassment and 50 percent experience unwanted sexual touching in their schools. One third of all girls report sexual rumors being spread about them, and one fourth report being cornered and molested... The classrooms and hallways of our schools are the most common sites for sexual harassment. Many girls are

afraid to speak up for fear of worse harassment." (See Suggested Reading, Pipher, pp.71–72.)

What Parents Can Do

Parents need to understand how social oppression works if they are to help a child who becomes a victim of prejudice, discrimination, or harassment. All three agents of social oppression support each other in a destructive way. Prejudice and discrimination can both be used to justify the existence of the other. Prejudice says: "Because you are inferior, you should not be allowed to do what the majority is free to do." (Therefore, discrimination is justified.) Discrimination says: "Because you don't do what the majority does, you must be inferior." (Therefore, prejudice is justified.) Harassment says: "You'd better shut up about what's happening or you'll get hurt worse." (Therefore, prejudice and discrimination remain unchallenged.) In addition, in a majority-run system, the minority victim often gets blamed ("She was asking for it, the way she was dressed") and the majority perpetrator often gets excused ("He's really a good kid, and after all, boys will be boys").

To grow up with some kind of minority status in a majority-run system often means that a child has to overcome social resistance from prejudice, discrimination, and harassment. Even when he or she establishes some degree of acceptance, achievement, or social position, however, the forces of social oppression can remain a fact of daily life. Majority prejudice, for example, may still do its demeaning work. "Her success just goes to show she's the exception to the rule—most minorities don't belong in that position." "The only reason he was chosen is because of receiving special treatment—if advantages weren't created in his favor, he'd never have been accepted." What parents can tell their minority child of whatever designation is this: "To do as well as a majority person in this world, the likelihood is that you will be judged by a higher standard, may have to work twice as hard, and may experience majority resentment for what you have been able to accomplish."

Should their child fall victim to *majority prejudice*, parents may need to give *psychological help*. "What they say about you is *not* about you, it is about them. It is about their ignorance or their desire to be mean." They can also repeat Eleanor Roosevelt's maxim: "No one can make you feel inferior without your consent."

Should their child fall victim to *majority discrimination*, parents may need to give advocacy help. "Your equal rights are being violated, and we will find someone to make a case to challenge the unfairness that is going on."

Should their child fall victim to *majority harassment*, parents may need to give *social help*. "We will speak to whatever authorities we must to get this treatment stopped and to create social safety for you at school."

If parents have had, or continue to have, their own minority experience with the three agents of social oppression, they can share with the child how they have learned to effectively deal with prejudice, discrimination, and harassment over the years.

Finally, there is this possibility: Schools in which intergroup prejudice, discrimination, and harassment run unchecked may risk provoking victims to strike back in violence to revenge mistreatment that authorities have chosen to allow.

23

DEPRESSION

WHEN SELF-WORTH IS LOST

The term *depression* refers to a severe state of despondency in which a person becomes emotionally stuck, typically feeling trapped in hurt, hopelessness, helplessness, and anger, without having much energy or motivation available to make any positive change. *One common by-product of this painful and impotent state is low self-esteem.*

Not too many years ago, the prevailing myth was that children don't get depressed. After all, what could they possibly have to get depressed about? Their lives are sheltered, simple, and easy. Their needs are taken care of. Their days are filled with play and fun. They are protected from the responsibilities of independence. They are spared the true hardships that adults know all too well. They aren't grown up enough to get really down. Right? No. Wrong on all counts. Childhood offers no immunity to the adversities of life and to the overwhelming demands that can contribute to becoming depressed. *Children are as susceptible to depression as adults.*

Childhood Depression

A high school student might *experience depression* after a recent escapade that cost playing for the varsity team, triggering additional social approval and status losses as well. Feeling overwhelmed by negative consequences, the despairing young person may attack *self-evaluation* with blame, punishing self-esteem: "I've just destroyed everything that mattered to me. I've disappointed everyone. I'm nothing but a failure!" *When regret, criticism, guilt, or shame gain control of self-perception, sense of worth is at serious risk of devastating harm.*

Unlike feeling sorrow, which has a transitory quality ("Unhappy things can get me down, but they can't keep me down"), experiencing depression has the hopeless, helpless feel of going on forever. Some common signs of depression to look for in children include the following behaviors:

- Withdrawal from friends
- Isolating and communicating less within the family
- Expressing significant unhappiness through words or tears
- No longer liking, even giving up, activities previously enjoyed
- Acting more angry and provoking more conflict in the family
- Getting into trouble at school or with the law
- Making global, self-critical statements
- Having difficulty sleeping
- Loss of humor
- Substance abuse
- No longer caring about personal appearance
- Loss of appetite, or eating all the time
- Showing a drop in school achievement
- Dramatic weight loss or gain
- Experiencing chronic fatigue
- Becoming increasingly pessimistic about the future
- Reckless behavior—fast driving, physical daring, sexual promiscuity

- Self-mutilation
- Preoccupation with the dark side of life in one's creative expression

Sexual Differences When Acting Depressed

Male and female children can be socialized quite differently around the management of emotion, particularly the management of pain, which girls may be encouraged to acknowledge and express and boys may be encouraged to deny and suppress. (The reverse is often the case around another emotion, *anger*, with boys allowing its expression, and girls often not.) Taught that it is womanly to be sensitive and vulnerable, a girl may directly show she is depressed. Taught that it is manly to be tough and act aggressive when hurt, a boy may only indirectly show he is depressed. Parents need to be sensitive to the differences, particularly with sons. "Because boys feel pressured to mask their genuine pain…recognizing sadness and depression in boys tends to be more difficult than recognizing them in girls." (See Suggested Reading, Pollack, pp. 311–313.)

Thus, on the lookout for *emotional signs of depression in their daughter*, parents might want to be more sensitive to: tearfulness, dejection, guilt, discouragement, disinterest, social withdrawal, self-criticism, apathy, defeatism, resignation, and worry. On the lookout for *emotional signs of depression in their son*, parents might want to be more sensitive to: anger, hostility, blame, cynicism, antagonism, social aggression, sarcasm, irritability, defiance, disobedience, and explosiveness.

What Causes Depression?

Depression is a complex condition having many possible factors that can contribute to its occurrence: genetic predisposition in the family; biochemical imbalance in the brain; early social deprivation; emotional, physical, or sexual abuse; cognitive distortion of reality; significant loss or reversal of fortune; undue pressure or stress; "or repeated blows to one's self-esteem." (See Suggested Reading, Pollack, p. 308.)

Because depression often overwhelms a person's capacity to cope and raises the risk of serious self-harm, parents are well advised to seek professional help should their child become so afflicted. Seeking help, they need to remember that depression is multiply determined, and so it can take considerable psychological and psychiatric time to identify the relevant factors.

In many cases today, effective treatment often requires finding the right combination of psychotherapy and antidepressant medication. The role of medication is usually twofold:

1. To reduce some of the acute symptoms of pain and anxiety
2. To thereby free up the depressed person's energies to learn, through psychotherapy, how to live more happily within himself or herself, with others, and with the world

Suicide and Violence to Others

The extreme risk of depression is that self-worth can sink so low that the young person may come to think that life is not worth living. At this point, self-destructive behavior can become an option for killing pain that he or she may be willing to consider. "One in four youngsters will experience a serious episode of depression by the time they reach their eighteenth birthday... The majority of children who try to kill themselves are seriously depressed... The rate of suicide among teens has more than doubled over the past thirty years, making suicide the second leading cause of death among children ages fifteen to nineteen." (See Suggested Reading, Fassler and Dumas, pp. 2–3.)

Although females attempt suicide more often than males, males complete suicide more often than females, perhaps because men tend to choose more immediately destructive means (guns, for example) than women (drugs, for example). Boys can also fall victim to a common cultural *male heroic.* This credo dictates that *to be a man, one must appear strong and act tough at all costs, remain silent about hurt feelings, keep one's problems to oneself, be self-sufficient, don't admit fear or act scared, never turn down a risk or dare, be able to drink as much or more than anyone else, be able to act out anger and not talk it out, don't show weakness by asking for help, prize personal pride over admitting human frailty, and prove oneself aggressive in competition sports (winning), collision sports (hitting), and killing sports (hunting).* Subscribing to this code of "manly" conduct, it is often very hard for many boys to find nonviolent, constructive ways to cope when significant hurt occurs.

One of the most common scenarios leading a young person to suicide unfolds as follows:

1. Getting into a *depressed state* from a performance failure or relationship loss (Therefore, parents need to take significant failures or losses seriously and encourage hurt feelings to be talked out.)

2. Withdrawing into *psychological or social isolation* to conceal lowered self-esteem (Therefore, parents need to increase their support and expressions of personal affirmation.)

3. Allowing *distorted thinking* to create an exaggerated picture of hopelessness and helplessness (Therefore, parents need to provide a realistic perspective.)

4. Resorting to *substance use* to self-medicate pain, thereby increasing the likelihood that impulse may rule

(Therefore, parents need to discourage resorting to alcohol and drugs and obtain outside counseling help if they are unable to help talk the suffering through.)

5. Having *access to a ready means to end suffering by ending life* (Therefore, parents need to secure all household means for inflicting serious self-harm.)

In depression, self-esteem falls perilously low. If normal sorrow does not go away and depressive signs begin to appear, parents should seek a psychiatric or psychological evaluation of the situation. It is better to err on the side of too much caution than of too much hope.

Finally, not all violence from depression is suicidal. It can be abusively, even murderously, directed outward, *particularly by males, who are responsible for the vast majority of violent crimes.* To the depressed young mind, the worth of life (one's own or someone else's) can become reduced. Then, killing self or others may be seen as a viable way of revenging hurt or ending unendurable pain.

24

SUBSTANCE ABUSE AND ADDICTION

WHEN SELF-MEDICATION INJURES SELF-ESTEEM

According to national surveys conducted annually by the University of Michigan, by the end of high school, most teenagers have had some level of substance use. At what age this substance use begins is extremely important, because the earlier in adolescence it starts, the greater likelihood of drug abuse and drug addiction problems later on. Therefore, it is definitely worthwhile for parents to do what they can, with persuasion and prohibition, to play for as much delay as they can get. *The later that substance use begins, the less chance there is for harmful involvement to occur.*

Among adolescents, the drugs most commonly selected are inhalants, nicotine, alcohol, and marijuana. The gateway drug is usually nicotine, with teenage smokers far more likely to experiment with other drugs and to become harmfully involved with alcohol than teenagers who elect not to smoke (according to the 1998 National Household Survey on Drug Abuse).

Levels of Substance Use

There are *five levels of drug use* for parents to beware, none of which are safe, but which get progressively more serious as they proceed: *experimental use*, *recreational use*, *excessive use*, *abusive use*, and *addictive use.* Although the first three levels carry some level of physical risk, the last two can be particularly damaging to self-esteem. How are these levels of use defined?

- Level one, *experimental use*, means trying a given substance no more than several times to see what the experience is like. Curiosity satisfied, there is no further need or want to use. "I tried pot and it didn't do anything for me."
- Level two, *recreational use*, means sometimes electing to enjoy a substance in social company, doing so in moderation (so that in one's own and other people's estimation, no problems are created), and retaining sufficient self-awareness to accurately monitor the affects of use. "I'll have one or two beers when I go out with my friends, enough to loosen up but not so much I lose touch with what's going on."
- Level three, *excessive use*, means occasionally using to the degree that sobriety is lost, with the young person becoming intoxicated. "Sometimes the fun of drinking is getting drunk."

For a significant percentage of teenagers, these first three levels describe the extent of their chemical use. For another percentage, however, one or two more serious levels of involvement can occur: *substance abuse* and even *addiction.* Why some young people who use substances manage to avoid these last two levels of involvement and others do not, is not precisely known. A family history of chemical dependency in one or two preceding generations has been associated with the increased likelihood that a child may have problems with substances. Genetic inheritance and perhaps social learning appear to play some part in this vulnerability. In any case, *when a child abuses drugs or becomes drug addicted, self-esteem usually becomes adversely affected.*

Substance Abuse and Self-Esteem

Substance abuse, level four, means use that is characterized by *two harmful effects*: *loss of traditional caring results* and *bad (problem-causing) decisions are made* as a consequence of use. Both effects injure self-esteem.

1. *Loss of traditional caring.* If substance abuse has a motivation, it seems to be to gain *freedom from care.* "I don't care about what I used to like or believe." "I don't care about how I affect others or what others think." "I don't care about how or what I do." "I don't care about fitting in or following rules." "I don't care about what happens later."

   Because maintaining self-esteem requires treating oneself and one's life with care because they are considered worthwhile, this abandonment of caring usually lowers both self-definition ("I gave up a lot of things that really mattered") and self-evaluation ("I stopped thinking well of myself").

2. *Making decisions that cause problems.* As traditional caring is lost, a host of ultimately harmful decisions can be made. There can be lying to get away with the forbidden and to escape consequences. There can be breaking rules at home and at school, and laws out in the world. There can be engaging in reckless risk taking. There can be talking to and treating loved ones in hurtful ways. There can be allowing impulse and immediate gratification to rule judgment. There can be letting school performance go, defaulting on commitments, and quitting jobs.

   As problems from poor choices mount, self-image and self-worth tend to decline. "I've screwed up again. Everyone's on my case. I can't do anything right!"

Finally, the two hallmarks of substance abuse—loss of caring and poor decision making—can interlock. As freedom from care creates unmindfulness of consequences, bad decisions may increase. And as bad decisions increase, not caring may become a way to live with the increasingly negative costs.

To help break the cycle of substance abuse, parents must encourage the child to assume *responsibility* because that road leads back to decisions based on self-respect and traditional caring. They can encourage growth of responsibility at this juncture in a couple of ways, neither of which is likely to earn them much gratitude from their son or daughter at the time.

They can allow the child to face and recover from the consequences of his or her bad decisions, and not excuse or provide rescue from problems caused. And, they can restrict significant social freedoms, requiring the child to earn those freedoms back by demonstrating more responsible behavior at home, at school, and out in the world.

Addiction and Self-Esteem

Addiction, level five, means coming to compulsively depend upon the self-destructive use of a substance to survive. What *enables* the self-destruction of dependency is *denial*, so expressions of denial are one good indicator of addiction. "It's not a problem, and besides, I can stop any time I want." What *justifies* the self-destruction of dependency is *resentment*, so expressions of resentment are another good indicator of addiction. "Anyone would get drunk if they had to put up with everything I have to." Two components of drug dependence do great harm to self-esteem: *loss of control* and *self-defeating behavior*.

1. *Loss of control*. By the time a young person has made the journey from experimental use to

recreational use, to excessive use, to substance abuse, and finally to substance addiction, a reversal of control has taken place. At the beginning, the person's elective choice determined consumption of the substance, but at the end, the person's physical and psychological craving has come to dictate use.

Despite what denial insists, stopping what has now become a self-destructive habit can be overwhelmingly difficult. Rationalization keeps promising just one more time will be the last, but resolve to quit proves no match for the compulsion to continue. Power of want defeats willpower time and time again. As the addicted young person feels increasingly unable to resist the lure of drugs to feel good or to stop feeling bad, life becomes increasingly unmanageable. Against better judgment and in the face of increasing problems, he or she still continues to use. Feeling increasingly at the drug's mercy, *loss of control over one's life lowers self-esteem.* "I have no willpower. I'm weak. I'm a failure. I hate myself for living in this helpless way."

2. *Self-defeating behaviors.* In recovery, what most addicted young people learn is that dependency on the substance is now the least of their problems. What they discover is that in living the addictive lifestyle, dedicating most of their daily energies toward satisfying their craving, they became habituated in another way they did not suspect. They became reliant on a set of behaviors that supported the addiction, behaviors that now become self-defeating in recovery. A few common self-defeating behaviors that are often a by-product of addictive living are:

- *Avoiding problems* instead of encountering problems
- *Getting by* instead of setting future goals
- *Procrastinating* instead of taking timely action
- *Going to extremes* instead of practicing moderation
- *Valuing excitement* instead of appreciating the ordinary
- *Gratifying impulse* instead of delaying or denying gratification
- *Conning people* to get needs met instead of being nonmanipulative
- *Making excuses* instead of taking responsibility
- *Breaking commitments* instead of keeping promises
- *Not finishing initiatives* instead of completing what one starts
- *Lying to oneself and others* instead of facing the truth and being honest
- *Storing up grievances with blame* instead of working to free oneself of resentment

Self-defeating behaviors lower self-esteem. "I don't get it. I've stopped using, but my life isn't getting any better. I'm just spinning my wheels." Sobriety requires getting abstinent, but *recovery* demands something more: *learning to live within oneself, with others, and with the world in self-enhancing ways.*

Should their child get involved with substances to the point of addiction, in-patient or out-patient treatment is usually worth a try—to create a period of forced abstinence, to assess the damage done, to begin to heal hurt family relationships, and perhaps to commit to a path of recovery. Treatment or not, most addicted people of any age need the help of Alcoholics Anonymous or Narcotics Anonymous (see local phone directory for numbers) to support continued abstinence and provide guidance for recovery. Parents themselves usually benefit from attending Al-Anon (also in local phone directory) to help them identify and give up well-meaning behaviors that have usually enabled their child's destructive use and caused them to act in self-destructive ways themselves.

Recovery from both substance abuse and addiction is always about the recovery of self-esteem.

25

ABANDONMENT AND ABUSE

WHEN COMMITMENT FAILS

High among the needs that children have to feel secure in the family are:

- *Trust in parental constancy* (the confidence that parents will not *abandon* them)
- *Safety in parental care* (the confidence that parents will not *abuse* them)

When either of these commitments is broken, not only can the child feel frightened ("What's going to happen to me now?") and betrayed ("Parents shouldn't act this way!"), but the boy or girl is also at risk of suffering both short- and long-term blows to self-esteem.

In the short term, both abandonment and abuse can cause feelings of *rejection.* Abandonment can feel like a rejection of worth ("I didn't matter enough for my dad to stay around") and abuse can feel deserved ("If I wasn't such a bad person, my mom wouldn't have treated me so badly").

In the long term, both abandonment and abuse can cause the child (or even later as an adult) to keep himself or herself from getting what is dearly wanted (a constant, safe, caring relationship) by self-protecting: sacrificing further human closeness for the sake of avoiding further hurt. This *fear of commitment* can cause the child to:

- *Keep distant* and stay uninvolved
- *Leave relationships* at the slightest hint of harm, or provoke an incident that justifies leaving
- *Stay in control* of any significant relationship by dictating the terms

Behind each of these strategies for survival is the belief that all caring relationships are inherently unreliable and dangerous, and so merit *distrust.* In consequence, children of abandonment or abuse may approach later relationships in a manner that is often *self-defeating.* To reduce the risks of harm, they may deny themselves the rewards of committed relationships they long to have. As adults who have suffered abandonment or abuse as children, they may resolve: "I'm not going to allow anyone to get close enough to hurt me again."

Abandonment and Self-Esteem

For a child, abandonment is the experience of being left by a significant loved one, usually a parent, who to some significant degree is "not there" to count on to be an integral part of the boy's or girl's life as much as before. It creates *the abiding and painful sense of absence.*

Abandonment can occur as a function of *death:* a parent prematurely stricken with a fatal disease, for example. It can occur as a function of *disability:* a parent becomes seriously physically or mentally ill. It can occur as a function of *divorce:* a noncustodial parent moves away and becomes less available. It can occur as a function of *dislocation:* a family moves with such frequency that children feel constantly uprooted. It can occur as a function of *desertion:* a parent exits family responsibility and cuts off contact with children. It can occur as a function of *disinterest:* a parent becomes self-absorbed in a new job, relationship, or addiction at the expense of the family.

In addition to causing children to feel bereft, rejected, or neglected at the immediate time, *abandonment can affect children's self-definition.* Social identity substantially depends on whom a person feels connected to: "My family is a lot of who I am." Abandonment, by reducing that sense of connection, can diminish self-esteem. The child can feel "less than" he or she was before—less complete, because a valued part of self has been taken away. "I don't have what I had with Mom now that she's got my stepfather." "Not having Dad as a regular part of my life makes him and me not the same." "Every time we move, I have to leave part of myself behind."

Older children who have experienced abandonment sometimes describe their state of being as "something missing" or "having a hole inside to fill." Unhappily, some of them strive to compensate for this in self-defeating ways: through frantic busyness, through insatiable hunger for material possessions, through serial relationships that never seem to last, even through substance use to escape the hollowness within.

Living in a culture wed to constant change does not help. The fickleness of fashion, how goods are made to be disposable, marital instability, technological innovation, and public discontent with the status quo all make it hard for anyone growing up in this country, much less a child of abandonment, to find a caring relationship to count on. How people treat things seems similar to how they treat each other: *everyone like everything is made to be replaceable.*

Sometimes, parents can help children suffering from abandonment by stating: "Certain things about you can never be taken from you by anyone else: your character, your capacities, and your choice to love yourself. Abandonment by other people cannot take you away from you." In addition, some parents, who by religious faith are so inclined, can say: "If all the people who love you, and all their love, were suddenly taken away, you could still count on being loved. By the very fact that you are God's creation, you are loved."

Recovery from abandonment requires rebuilding faith in the constancy of caring relationships. What is usually required is not therapy but *therapeutic relationships* with transitional commitment figures (significant friends, teachers, mentors, extended family members), in relationship to whom a young person gradually learns to trust and commit again.

Abuse and Self-Esteem

As in helping, so in parenting, the first rule is: *try to do no harm.* Abuse is behavior by parents that inflicts significant injury to children. It can be *verbal:* attacking insecurity with sarcastic words, for example. It can be *emotional:* battering with unrelenting or threatening anger, for example. It can be *physical:* expressing frustration with blows or beating into submission, for example. It can be *sexual:* expressing carnal interest or taking carnal gratification, for example.

In addition to causing children grievous harm at the immediate time, *abuse can affect children's self-evaluation* when they blame or shame themselves for the mistreatment that occurred. Why would they blame themselves? Because the parent may blame them to escape responsibility: "You made me do that!" Or, they may assume unloving treatment from a parent could only occur if it was deserved: "I'm not worth loving." As for shame, it follows blame: "I feel disgraced."

Whether abuse is occasional or continual, children must struggle to understand how someone who is supposed to love them could treat them in such unloving, hurtful ways. To create an explanation, they will often implicate themselves in what occurred.

Thus, an abused child, wanting desperately to believe that he or she has a loving parent despite evidence to the contrary, may judge himself or herself harshly by the following kinds of thinking: "I am not worth treating well." "I had this coming." "I am at fault for how they acted." "To be treated better, I must work harder at being a better person."

Thus, in response to sexual abuse by a trusted family member, a young girl explains: "I got myself raped." Partly this statement may reflect insufficient self-esteem to place responsibility where it belongs, partly it may reflect disbelief that such a violation could happen without it being earned, and partly it may reflect a desperate attempt to claim some control over an experience she was otherwise powerless to prevent. Recovery from such a violation includes coming to disown responsibility for mistreatment received so that self-blame does not do ongoing damage to self-esteem.

No child is at fault for being abused. Thus, after one parent loses physical control to get control of an argument with a defiant adolescent, the other parent may say to the teenager: "Even though you repeatedly refused to do what was wanted, that's no excuse for how you were treated. No child deserves to be hit." Then to the spouse: "You have to find nonviolent ways to manage disagreements in this family."

For the abusive parent to forsake his or her harmful ways, counseling can often be of substantial help in speeding along the process of necessary change. The key to this behavior change is *practice*, through conscious effort replacing an old way of acting and reacting with a new way, until the new becomes more natural than the old.

Reducing Risk of Sexual Abuse

To reduce the risk of sexual abuse, any nonmarital feelings of sexual temptation toward other members of the family must be taken seriously and counseling should be sought right away. To delay getting help increases the risk that a child or stepchild, brother or sister, will receive an injury that may be beyond emotional repair. The parent to whom a child reports sexual abuse needs to believe the boy or girl enough to get the report immediately evaluated by a counselor who knows enough to confirm or disconfirm the accusation. *A parent who denies the sexual abuse of another family member becomes complicit in the violation that has occurred.*

For the abused child, recovery requires restoring faith in one's capacity to set safe boundaries in caring relationships as well as to have them respected, and to have choices to self-protect or leave should abuse ever appear likely to recur.

26

CHARACTER AND SELF-ESTEEM

LIVING ON GOOD TERMS WITH ONESELF

What is *character*, and why is it important to a person's self-esteem? Character is a combination of belief and action. It is a combination of whatever rules of right conduct one is taught and the willingness to put those rules into practice in daily life. To exercise character requires *integrity*—committing to make decisions and take actions that are consistent with one's ethical beliefs.

A person of strong character has the integrity to live by his or her moral convictions

- *Within oneself* (acting *responsibly* and *honestly*, for example)
- *With others* (treating people with *compassion* and *respect*, for example)
- *With the world* (taking stands for *equity* and *justice*, for example)

Beliefs about right conduct that provide the foundation of a child's character come from many sources. They are taught by parents by instruction and example, by religious faith, by formal education, by popular culture, and by social experience, particularly by the influence of peers. Obviously, not all externally derived beliefs are consistent with those taught at home, and when they are not, parents need to speak up and reassert their values. In doing so, their goal is not to argue to change their child's mind, but rather to present their own perspective for discussion so the child can appreciate what they stand for on this issue and why. If they want the child to reconsider, they must do so without putting him or her on the defensive: "I know you thought the violence in the film was funny. I'd like to tell you why I did not."

Some ethical diversity inevitably exists between one generation and the next in every family. This is not from want of character so much as from growing up under different circumstances in a changing time. Parents who believe in tithing to give to others less fortunate, for example, may have grown children who believe in investing all of what they earn in their immediate household.

In addition, part of the larger social diversity also includes diversity in ethical creeds. Thus, one culture may believe it is right to revenge historical wrongs and maintain hostilities toward traditional enemies, for example, whereas another may believe it is right to forgive past offenses and make peace with former adversaries. *Character is more dependent on the exercise of integrity (matching actions with ethics) than on any one specific set of values and beliefs.*

Conscience and Self-Esteem

If integrity is what supports character by keeping decisions and actions in accord with one's personal ethics, then *conscience* is what allows integrity to chart its moral course. In doing so, *conscience has enormous influence on self-esteem.*

When children act out of integrity, their behavior is consistent with their ethical beliefs, their conscience approves their conduct, they can feel good about themselves, and their self-esteem is raised. "I'm proud of what I chose to do." "I'm glad that I spoke up." "I did the right thing for refusing to do wrong." When children choose *not* to act out of integrity, their behavior violates their ethics, their conscience disapproves (despite any momentary pleasure gained), they can feel bad about themselves, and their self-esteem is lowered. "I wish I hadn't done that." "I wish I hadn't said that." "I wish I'd had the courage to say 'No.'"

This last statement is worth reflecting on because *acts of character are very often acts of courage.* A child is brave enough to stand up against temptation. A child is brave enough to refuse to go along. A child is brave enough to state an unpopular belief. A child is brave enough to choose the harder and longer path, instead of taking a shortcut to the easy way out.

Whenever parents see their child showing character by acting out of integrity, according to conscience, at some personal expense for what he or she believes is right, they need to recognize the courage such decision making takes, and they need to reinforce the benefit to his or her self-esteem. "Making right choices in life is often not easy, but when you do, you bring out the best in yourself. By acting according to your beliefs, you end up with a good opinion of yourself, and that's what having strong self-esteem is all about."

Adolescence as a Test of Character

Adolescence continually tests a teenager's character around common rules of conduct learned as a child that he or she is now tempted to violate.

- A teenager may be tempted *to lie* for freedom's sake, to do the forbidden or to keep from getting caught. Weighing the desire for ill-gotten freedom against the desire to remain honestly connected to parents is a common test of adolescent character.
- A teenager may be tempted *to deny personal responsibility,* by making excuses or casting blame to avoid facing the

consequences of a bad decision. Weighing the desire to escape accountability against assuming ownership for what one chose to do is a common adolescent test of character.

- A teenager may be tempted *to give up valued goals*, in order to avoid hard work he or she does not enjoy. Weighing the rewards of persistence against freedom from effort is a common adolescent test of character.

One role of parents during their son's or daughter's adolescence is to hold the teenager to ethical account for those rules of conduct that he or she learned as a child. At issue is not castigating, shaming, or provoking guilt in the young person when a lack of character is shown. Rather, the parent's role is to provide a moral compass when temptation makes it easy for a teenager to fall away from doing what he or she believes is right, and in doing so risk injuring his or her self-esteem.

To help the adolescent meet this test of character, some old notions often bear repetition.

- Don't compromise yourself, because you're all you've got.
- Treat yourself right by acting right as often as you can.
- To be content with yourself, be true to what you believe and be truthful to others.
- Don't confuse character and reputation: the first you control, the second you do not.
- There are two sources of happiness—from getting what you want and from doing what is right, and the second lasts far longer than the first.

27

EMOTIONS AND SELF-ESTEEM

FEELINGS AS GOOD INFORMANTS BUT BAD ADVISERS

Human beings are given many *ways of knowing* about themselves and their life experience.

- They can be *intuitive*, sensing the mechanics of how things work, for example.
- They can be *spiritual*, connecting with a universal presence for enlightenment, for example.
- They can be *physical*, seeing or touching their surroundings, for example.
- They can be *intellectual*, thinking about what occurred, for example.
- They can be *emotional*, feeling their response to an event, for example.

These are all vital capacities that allow people to become informed about their inner and outer worlds. Emotional knowing, just like the other kinds, can contribute to confidence: "I know what's going on." *Understanding what one is feeling can strengthen self-esteem by adding a measure of control:* "I'm feeling disappointed and just want to be alone for awhile." Ignorance often has the opposite effect, creating confusion: "I don't know what's the matter with me!"

Feelings as Good Informants

Emotions *inform* people about their felt response to a significant life experience and energize them to respond. Emotions can empower a person to make an expressive response ("I feel angry"), or a corrective response ("Please don't do that again"), or a protective response ("I'm going to report what you did"). Because of their informing and energizing properties, emotions are always worth listening and attending to. In one form or another, they all say: "Be alert, something important is happening in my life right now, something that may merit a response."

Although feelings are neither good nor bad, people tend to assign them that distinction based on how the emotion is experienced. Thus, "good" emotions may include pride (focusing on accomplishment), love (focusing on devotion), joy (focusing on fulfillment), interest (focusing on attraction), or gratitude (focusing on appreciation). In general, people are happy to experience these and other positive feelings. "Bad" emotions, by contrast, are unhappy to experience, and may include fear (focusing on danger), pain (focusing on injury), grief (focusing on loss), anger (focusing on violation), or frustration (focusing on blockage).

Emotional Education

Children need to be taught how to recognize, label, talk about, and manage feelings so that their emotions work for, not against, them. Parents are responsible for this emotional education that can include the following components.

1. To foster *emotional awareness*, parents can teach sensitivity through listening. "When you are feeling troubled by something strong inside but don't know what it is, try becoming quiet and paying close attention to yourself. Maybe you can hear an inner voice or see an image that will tell you what is emotionally

going on. It takes practice to recognize what your feelings are."

2. To foster *emotional trust*, parents can validate the child's ultimate authority on knowing what he or she is feeling. "It is no one else's business to decide what you are feeling or to tell you that you should or shouldn't feel a certain way. Whether or not you or other people like them, your feelings need to be accepted for what they are."

3. To foster *emotional literacy*, parents can teach their child to attach descriptive labels—words, phrases, images—to capture their emotional state in verbal terms. "Once you learn how to put your feelings into words, then you can describe your emotions to someone else."

4. To foster *emotional communication*, parents can teach the child that by discussing feelings, many problems in life can be worked out. "If you can tell me what I did that got you started feeling this way, then maybe I can do something different the next time so this unhappiness doesn't happen for you again."

Feelings as Bad Advisers

Emotions, particularly of the unhappy kind, can create a special jeopardy for a child's self-esteem. The reason for this risk is that *although emotions are very good informants, they can be very bad advisers.* When the child allows unhappy feelings to "think" for him or her, often what he or she "feels" is best to do in order to make things better is often exactly what will make things worse. *The emotional state is being allowed to determine the cognitive choice.*

Consider just a few common examples.

- *Depression* counsels: "be inactive," instead of getting active on one's own behalf to make things better.
- *Discouragement* counsels: "look at all the negative," instead of looking for the positive to make things better.
- *Anger* counsels: "revenge," instead of finding a constructive way to address the wrong to make things better.
- *Fear* counsels: "run away," instead of standing and facing the threat to make things better.
- *Helplessness* counsels: "give up," instead of keeping trying to make things better.
- *Loneliness* counsels: "withdraw," instead of reaching out to make things better.
- *Shyness* counsels: "be silent," instead of speaking up to make things better.
- *Shame* counsels: "be secret," instead of openly communicating to make things better.

In order for children to treat emotions as good servants that support self-esteem and not bad masters that can injure it, they need to be taught this distinction: *"Use your feelings to become informed, but use your thinking to decide what to do."*

28

THINKING AND SELF-ESTEEM

MAKING UP ONE'S MIND

As suggested in the preceding Key, children's self-esteem can benefit when they are taught to accept their feelings as good informants, even when the emotional news is bad—"I'm feeling lonely," "I'm feeling disappointed," "I'm feeling embarrassed."

Emotions speak the truth of the moment, and this self-awareness, even when unhappy, *validates* the child's experience: "I'm worried about what might happen." Emotional pretense or lying estranges the child from himself or herself: "I'm not afraid of anything!" It is hard to feel connected to oneself and good about oneself when one denies oneself. Such dishonesty is one enemy of self-esteem, causing people to conceal from others or themselves the reality of how they actually are.

How Thought Can Be Independent of Feeling

As also previously mentioned, children's self-esteem can benefit when they are taught that feeling bad does not have to impel behaviors that lead to feeling worse. Knowing that feelings can be bad advisers, children can use their *power of thought* (of understanding and reason) to act in ways that alleviate suffering—socially reaching out to overcome loneliness, doing something enjoyable to make up for disappointment, or objecting to teasing to reduce embarrassment.

Children can be taught to overrule advice from their heart with judgment from their head.

How Feeling Can Depend on Thought

Thought cannot only provide a restraint on emotional advice, it can influence the nature of emotional experience as well. Understanding this connection, children can take an active role in actually affecting how they feel. Consider three ways this can be done.

1. They can choose *how to believe about themselves.* There is an enormous emotional difference between believing "I am okay as I am" (feeling worthy) or "I will never be good enough" (feeling deficient).

2. They can choose *how to interpret adverse events.* There is an enormous emotional difference between interpreting someone's undesirable action as "They weren't paying attention" (feeling objective) or as "They did that on purpose to get me" (feeling grievance).

3. They can choose *how to forecast the future.* There is an enormous emotional difference between anticipating "Better things may happen if I just keep trying" (feeling hopeful) or "Nothing will work out no matter what I do" (feeling hopeless).

Positive or negative thinking can powerfully influence self-esteem. Negative thinking can foster worry, pessimism, apathy, and inaction. Positive thinking can encourage confidence, optimism, enthusiasm, and effort. As Abraham Lincoln once said: "People are about as happy as they make up their minds to be."

The Management of Meaning

Thus, children can learn about the consequences of each kind of thought and can be taught how to make up their minds. When a boy or girl experiences an unwanted event or outcome, parents can listen for the beliefs, interpretations, and forecasts that their son or daughter is using to construe what has just happened. For example, they can attend what *meaning* the child chooses to give to not making a team, after the disappointment has been felt.

	Negative meaning would be:	*Positive meaning* would be:
Belief:	"I'm a lousy athlete."	"I got beaten out by better competition."
Interpretation:	"No one would want me on their team."	"I tried my best."
Forecast:	"I'll never do sports again."	"I'm going to find another way to play."

Parents have a very significant role in helping their child come to terms with ordinary hardship. Because *perception can mediate emotion*, they need to monitor the meaning the child attaches to what happened. If they see the child using positive thinking to support his or her self-esteem in the aftermath of adversity, they need to reinforce that mental attitude. If they see their child using negative thinking, they need to point out the choice the child is making and the emotional consequences that follow, and suggest alternative ways for understanding what has occurred.

They can explain to their child: "Your emotional state partly depends on what you choose to believe about yourself, how you choose to interpret the experience, and how you choose to forecast what is likely to happen now. Therefore, whenever you are feeling upset about anything, it is always worthwhile asking yourself this question: 'What am I thinking?' *A lot of times, all it takes to change how you feel, is to change your mind.*" Then give a technique for changing one's mind. "People talk to themselves silently all the time. This is called *self-talk.* So if you are feeling unhappy, check out what you are saying to yourself. If you discover a lot of discouraging self-talk going on inside your head, interrupt that dialogue with encouraging self-talk instead. Then keep that positive self-talk up until you start to feel better."

29

EXPECTATIONS AND SELF-ESTEEM

ANTICIPATION, MOTIVATION, AND ADEQUACY

- When a child can *accurately anticipate reality*, and not be totally caught unawares by what occurs, a *sense of control* is gained.
- When a child can *positively motivate his or her own performance*, and not give up the desire to try, a *sense of purpose* is gained.
- When a child can *live on terms of self-acceptance* and not feel threatened when personal standards of conduct are not met, *a sense of contentment* is gained.

All these gains tend to enhance a child's sense of self-esteem, and they depend upon how that boy or girl has learned to manage *expectations* in a variety of ways.

What Expectations Are

Expectations are mental sets that people create for two purposes.

1. To *frame the reality* in which they live to give themselves a sense of reference: "I'm doing what is expected of me."
2. To *prepare for reality* to come: "This is what I expect is going to happen."

Without benefit of any expectations, people can feel disorientated in the present ("I have no idea what I'm supposed to be doing") and fearful of a future that is unknown ("I haven't a clue to what this experience is going to be like").

There are three common kinds of expectations that a child relies on to establish a frame of reference in the present and to anticipate the future.

- *Predictions*—what the boy or girl believed *would* happen or believes *will* happen. "I will pass this test."
- *Ambitions*—what the boy or girl *wanted* or *wants* to happen. "I want to be chosen to be a class officer."
- *Conditions*—what the boy or girl thinks *should have* happened or *ought to* happen. "I should get more freedom than my little brother because I'm older."

Because expectations are chosen and not inherited, are flexible and not fixed, *a child can be taught how to create expectations that work for personal benefit and do not do personal harm.*

Expectations to Accurately Anticipate Reality

When the child chooses expectations that fit the reality of what occurs, a degree of affirmation is the usual outcome. So, when a *prediction* is met and the child passes the test, the boy or girl tends to feel *secure.* When an *ambition* is met and the child is chosen class officer, the boy or girl tends to feel *fulfilled.* And when a *condition* is met and the older child is given more freedom than the younger, the boy or girl tends to be *satisfied. Mental sets have emotional consequences*, and when the positive expectations people create fit the reality they encounter, good feelings usually follow and self-esteem is enhanced.

Conversely, when a child creates a set of expectations that are unrealistic, that do not fit the reality he or she anticipated, then violated expectations often create an unhappy response and self-esteem can be diminished. When the child fails the test (when passing was predicted), he or she feels surprised and experiences *anxiety:* "I don't understand how I could have done so badly!" When the child fails to be chosen class officer (when election was what was wanted), he or she feels disappointed and experiences *sadness:* "I really feel let down for not getting elected." When the child is not given any more freedom than a younger sibling (when different treatment seemed only just), he or she feels betrayed and experiences *anger:* "It's not fair that we get to do the same when I am so much older!"

When parents see their child choosing a set of expectations that do not accurately fit how things are or are likely to be, they can suggest revising those expectations in a more realistic way. *Parents have an important educational role in teaching the child to develop expectations that realistically fit the present and anticipate changes that are going to occur.* Thus, preparing their elementary schoolchild for middle school, they may say: "To help you learn more independence and responsibility, middle school teachers are likely to be more strict and less supportive than teachers in elementary school. So, you can probably *expect* that you *will* be told a lot of things only one time (prediction), that you may get less individual attention than you *want* (ambition), and that you will not be given second chances when you feel you *should* (condition)."

For anyone, child or adult, *to persist in holding expectations that do not fit reality sets up a person for continual violation from surprise and anxiety, from disappointment and sadness, from betrayal and anger.* Thus, the young man, who expects his ex-girlfriend to return when she has made it very plain that the romance is over, prolongs his unhappiness by refusing to accept what he cannot change. Over time, he only feels progressively worse, and that includes feeling worse about himself.

Clinging to *unrealistic expectations can also be used to rationalize unhealthy behavior* by denying the truth of what is actually going on. Thus, a high school sophomore, in her first romance, may create expectations that accept abusive treatment from an older guy. Frantic parents, not wanting their daughter to keep getting hurt, run into a wall of unrealistic expectations when they express their concerns. This is how the young woman defends her determination to stay in love.

- Her *prediction* based on fear is: "If I lose this relationship, I'll be so worthless I *will* never find another love."
- Her *ambition* based on hope is: "I *want* to believe the most recent act of abuse is the last and, with my love, from now on he will change for the better."
- Her *condition* based on guilt is: "This is my fault because I *should* be able to please him and be a good enough person so this abuse wouldn't be happening."

Mental sets have behavioral consequences. People occasionally use unrealistic expectations to justify and allow misconduct to occur. Parents can explain to their child a critical distinction: "*Although it is important to have expectations that fit the way things are (to accept what you cannot change), it is also sometimes important to adjust the way things are to fit a healthy set of expectations (to change what you can).*" Then they can suggest what such a healthy set of expectations might be: "In a healthy love relationship, you can expect to like how you treat yourself, to like how you treat the other person, and to like how that person treats you in return."

Expectations to Motivate Performance

Expectations can also serve to motivate (or de-motivate) performance. This is why so much of athletic coaching is headwork, not just bodywork. It is the art of getting players into a motivated or winning state of mind—believing they *can do*, as opposed to believing they cannot. One job of a parent is to teach children how to motivate themselves to maintain well-being, to meet challenges, and to pursue important goals. To do so, they can explain how mental sets, like expectations, have motivational consequences. They can describe the power of encouraging and discouraging expectations.

	Encouraging expectations:	Discouraging expectations:
Prediction:	"I *will* be able to succeed."	"I *will* never succeed."
Ambition:	"I *want* to achieve my goals."	"I don't *want* to try."
Condition:	"I *should* give it all I can."	"I *should* just give up."

Encouraging expectations inspire effort, improve the possibility of a desirable outcome, and, in the process, affirm self-esteem. Discouraging expectations reduce effort, increase the likelihood of a negative outcome, and, in the process, erode self-esteem. Parents can explain to their child: "*Believe in positive possibilities for yourself and you are more likely to work to make your aspirations and your dreams come true.*"

Expectations and Adequacy

There is a powerful question parents can ask their child: "*Who is the most important person for you to work to please?*" At first, the child may mention *external authorities* like parents or teachers. But that is not who parents mean. They want the child to be aware of the *internal authority* whose expectations count most of all—the authority of *the child's own expectations for personal adequacy.* And they want to help the child discriminate between self-expectations that provide a sense of acceptance and those that foster a sense of insufficiency. *Adequacy expectations create the inner terms on which a child lives within himself or herself on a daily basis.*

	Expectations of acceptance:	Expectations of insufficiency:
Prediction:	"I *will* do what I can."	"I *will* never do enough."
Ambition:	"I *want* what I have."	"I *want* as much as everybody else."
Condition:	"I *should* be as I am."	"I *should* be as others would like."

Expectations of acceptance create an inner world of self-content that contributes to peace of mind and affirms self-esteem: "I am grateful for being the individual I am." Expectations of insufficiency create an inner world of dissatisfaction that can generate ongoing stress and undermine self-esteem: "No matter how well I do or how much I have it is never good enough." Parents can explain to their child: *"You can set the terms on which you live within yourself by choosing expectations that affirm the adequacy of who and how you are and what you are able to do."*

Expectations are mental sets that a child can learn to create to benefit his or her self-esteem by:

- Using them *to accurately fit* and *anticipate reality*
- Using them *to positively motivate performance*
- Using them *to live on terms of acceptance within oneself*

30

STRESS AND SELF-ESTEEM

MAINTAINING ENERGY AND LIMITING CHANGE

By wearing down a person's sense of well-being, *stress can injure self-esteem* in four increasingly serious ways.

- Level one is *fatigue:* "I feel tired and discouraged most of the time." As weariness depletes energy, it depresses one's outlook, and *negativity can injure self-esteem.*
- Level two is *pain:* "I hurt a lot and can get easily upset." As suffering reduces one's resilience, *oversensitivity can injure self-esteem.*
- Level three is *burnout:* "I just don't seem to care anymore." As what meant a lot ceases to matter so much, *apathy can injure self-esteem.*
- Level four is *breakdown*: "I feel too bad to do what I should." As emotional or physical impairment limits normal capacity to perform, *inability to function injures self-esteem.*

Those parents who consider stress the exclusive by-product of becoming an adult wonder: what does stress have to do with children? In a way they are right, but they are also wrong.

Adults are largely susceptible to stress because of the demands of *independence.* There are a host of grown-up responsibilities to bear for themselves and, if they have a family, for others as well. Children, however, are largely susceptible to stress because of the demands of *dependence.* Having to live on terms set by a variety of adult authorities means not having control over many requirements and changes that rule their young lives.

What Stress Is

Stress is a *survival response* to what feels like a crisis or an overwhelming situation. It enables a person to generate emergency coping energy and hopefully survive. Triggered by a sense of threat, stress implies a scary question: "Can I cope with this challenge, and if I can't, what will happen to me?" Then, after the crisis has been resolved for good or ill, *the cost of stress must be paid.* Extreme expenditure of energy typically leaves a person's physical and emotional resources momentarily depleted, and he or she requires some rest and renewal to recover.

Overdemand

A common source of stress, both for adults and children, is *overdemand*—the experience of having more to do than time and energy available to get it done. Parents can explain the relationship between overdemand and stress this way.

- "For every demand placed upon you by circumstance, by somebody else, or by yourself, you must spend some unit of energy in response.
- "Energy is one's potential for doing or action, and it is *limited.* People do not possess this precious life resource in infinite supply.
- "As long as the demands upon you remain less than or equivalent to your readily available response energy, you will feel okay.

- "When those demands, however, exceed the supply of energy you readily have to give, then stress arises as you force your system to produce additional energy to survive the challenge at hand."

Procrastination

Parents can then illustrate the connection between overdemand and stress by describing a common source of self-induced stress familiar to most students. It is one that children create, and on which they often come to depend to get their schoolwork done: *procrastination*—the "put it off, pull it off" game.

For example, although the work was assigned two weeks ago, a student creates an emergency by not getting a project started until the night before it is due. What was a demand when first assigned now becomes an overdemand in consequence of the delay. Having *put it off* so long, stress will now be required to *pull it off* at the last minute. Energized by a sense of threat, and perhaps assisted by a stimulating chemical like caffeine, the young person stays up all night. Deadline pressure is used as motivation to overcome resistance to accomplishing an undesirable task. Stress has enabled the young person to get the job done, but not without paying a significant physical and emotional cost after the challenge has been met. There is some fatigue ("I feel worn-out"), and perhaps some pain ("I'm really irritable and I just want to be left alone!"). Because children have a tendency to avoid what is not fun to do, parents can at least explain why procrastination can be so expensive: "The longer you put something off, the more stressful energy will be required to finally get it done. It is the difference between doing work early and feeling calm and relaxed or doing work late, feeling anxious and rushed, and ending up exhausted."

Two Entries into Stress

If one entry into stress is through *overdemand*, the other is through *self-neglect*. In the first case, energy is overspent. In the second, it is undernourished. Parents can remind their child about *two laws of personal energy*. The first law (mentioned earlier) states: *personal energy is limited*, not inexhaustible. The second law states: *personal energy must be renewed* to remain in good supply. Violate the law of limitation with excessive demand or the law of renewal with neglect and stress is likely to result.

Maintenance and Self-Renewal

Parents can teach their child about renewal by clarifying and emphasizing the importance of *self-maintenance activities*. Maintenance activities may not be particularly interesting, fun to do, or exciting. They service an individual's recurring, basic needs so he or she can move from one day to the next with an adequate energy available to meet ordinary demands. Daily maintenance would include satisfying such common needs as having regular meals, good nutrition, basic hygiene, sufficient relaxation, loving contact with significant others, and adequate sleep. Neglect any of these and other maintenance needs for long enough and the child's system will run down, as adequate energy is now unavailable to meet normal daily demands. Should insufficient self-maintenance become protracted, then the boy or girl can express this deficit through the four signs of stress mentioned earlier: fatigue (feeling sluggish and sleepy), pain (acting cranky and tearful), burnout (being indifferent and passive), or breakdown (becoming quick to get sick and slow to recover). The self-esteem message is: "*One important way to keep feeling good about yourself is to keep taking regular care of yourself.*"

Demands for Change

If life were only a matter of meeting self-maintenance

demands, stress would be simpler to manage. Life, however, is more complicated than that. In addition to ongoing maintenance needs, there are also continual demands for *change.* A parent can give children *an operational definition for change* to help them identify when and where it is going on in their lives. "Change is occurring in your life any time there is the *start* of something new, there is the *end* of something old, there is an *increase* in the frequency or amount of what is happening, or there is a *reduction* in the frequency or amount of what is happening."

Many changes are *voluntary,* a child choosing them for personal satisfaction—*beginning* a new friendship, *stopping* an outgrown activity, getting *more* free time, having *fewer* social restrictions with older age. Most major life changes, however, are *nonvoluntary,* not what the child wants, not what the child can control. *Beginning* a new school because of a family move, *ending* a romantic relationship the other person has broken off, being given *more* responsibilities at home now that parents have divorced, or having *less* access to a custodial parent now that he or she has remarried.

Because *change* demands adjustment to altered circumstances, it takes *special effort,* not just ongoing effort as maintenance requires. Because it is more energy expensive than maintenance, *people have a limited tolerance for change,* typically the greatest cause of overdemand and stress in their lives. Understanding this, parents can urge children to limit change in their lives to an affordable amount. The self-esteem message is: "*One important way to feel good about yourself is to keep from overcommitting to too much change.*"

Why Children Become So Susceptible to Stress

It is hard for parents to teach children the importance of sufficient self-maintenance and the danger of excessive change because the boy or girl tends to value the first too little, and the second too much. From the child's point of view, maintenance often means just repeating the familiar, routine, same, old, boring things over and over again. Who wouldn't get tired of such ordinary demands, and where is the fun? Change, however, has a special allure to youth. It means experiencing unfamiliar, varied, different, new, exciting things for the first time. Who wouldn't prefer change with all its stimulation to the dull nourishment that maintenance provides?

Unhappily, here is where the marketplace weighs in with its relentless huckstering of change. Constantly offering, advertising, and glamorizing the latest fashion, the current entertainment, and the neatest toy, it relentlessly exploits young people's discontent with the old and hunger for the new. Children are sold on change without being told that *they have a limited tolerance for change*, and this can be to their later cost. Not having learned how to maintain basic health and how to resist the blandishments of excessive change, they may be at risk of growing into adulthood more prone to stress than protected from it. Their self-esteem may be at risk because they do too much to their cost and not enough to their benefit.

The self-esteem message is: "*The more voluntary and nonvoluntary change there is going on in your life, the more important it becomes to honor your self-maintenance needs for energy renewal.*"

How to Avoid Excessive Change

Parents can teach their child how to limit change by describing two kinds of hard choices, each of which requires using the same powerful word: "No."

1. Resisting excessive change demands can require *saying* "No" to others. "*If you go through life letting*

other people set your limits with their demands, you will keep setting yourself up for a lot of stress."

2. Resisting excessive change can also require *saying* "No" to one's self. "*If you let temptation set limits on your pleasure rather than using restraint to decide what is enough, you will end up paying for your fun with stress.*"

QUESTIONS AND ANSWERS

Do all cultures consider strong self-esteem to be a healthy trait?

Not necessarily. In fact, extremely communal cultures might believe the reverse, seeing this emphasis on the individual self as a threat to the collective good. Or consider how one of the world's major religions, Buddhism, preaches the negation of self and the desirability of transcending individuality to attain a higher level of spiritual awareness. *Simply because the concept of self-esteem is well regarded in one culture does not mean that it is universally valued.*

Is there any relationship between regular exercise and self-esteem?

Although our culture exalts a fit personal appearance through advertising and the popular media, by providing endless passive entertainment possibilities, it also encourages sedentary ways. Regular exercise helps *maintain* a person's sense of physical, emotional, and mental well-being (see Key 30.) In general, the more pillars of self-esteem that children have to depend on the better, and exercise is one that they can easily control. It literally allows them to invest in themselves for their own good, and to feel good about themselves for having done so.

Is being socially active good for a child's self-esteem?

By temperament, some children seem to be outgoing from a very early age, whereas others seem more socially reclusive and into themselves. A child can have strong self-esteem being introverted, enjoying solitary time, and having just a few good friends. There is, however, this to be said for *having a child active in as many social circles as possible*, be they neighborhood, extended family, church, sports, volunteer activity, special interest groups, or whatever. Particularly during the social cruelty years from late elementary to early middle school (see Key 17), it can really benefit a child to have outside circles of friends that are free from the politics of social meanness that often rule the harsh reality of classroom life. In that way, a bad day at school does not feel like the end of his or her social world.

Does sibling rivalry injure self-esteem?

That depends on how the rivalry is motivated and conducted. As a *friendly competition* that helps each child bring out the competitive best in the other, sibling rivalry can enhance self-esteem: "We push each other to do well." As a *ruthless conflict* where the objective is to assert dominance or superiority at all costs, however, sibling rivalry can injure self-esteem: "Making each other feel bad and look bad is what it's all about."

Sibling rivalry tends to be most intense when children are close in age and of the same sex. With insufficient differentiation between them, children will fight to win the battle of similarity the only way they can—by contesting who is better at how they both want to be (a shared self-definition). To reduce this rivalry, parents can try to substitute another goal: establishing how each is different from the other. Here the objective is to free up both children to develop individual interests and capacities unique to each of them. Supporting the development of natural diversity between the two can reduce pressure from social similarity and the intense rivalry it can create: "We get on so well because we're so different."

Can competition with parents injure self-esteem?

Yes, particularly when parents are the ones doing the competing, trying to keep up with the growing powers of their adolescent child. What powers? Of physical attractiveness, of athletic prowess, of worldly achievement, of personal happiness, of future opportunity, to name a few. It can be a hard reality for some parents to accept: in adolescence, the teenager's life is just beginning to open up just as parents are entering middle age and life is starting to close down. As they contemplate early signs of their own decline, they behold their teenager ascending into the fullness of young manhood or young womanhood. In response to this painful comparison, insecure parents can pick at or put down the teenager to reduce the threat they feel, and in the process damage the young man's or young woman's self-esteem. "No matter how I fix myself up, my mom always finds a way to criticize how I look." "Even though I tell him it's only a game, my dad gets really angry when he starts to lose."

In general, mothers and fathers are better served recognizing their jealousy for what it is—a natural envy arising from regret, not at what the teenager through growth has gained but at what the parents through aging have lost.

Can power struggles with a child lower parental self-esteem?

Yes, particularly if these conflicts result from trying to change what one cannot realistically control. Continual frustration and constant failure can create painful feelings of incompetence. To avoid such fruitless efforts, parents need to be able to discriminate between what in their child they can influence and what they cannot. One medical doctor's advice is helpful in this regard: "I have learned as a pediatrician, mother and grandmother that there are five things parents cannot make their child do: eat, poop, fall asleep, be happy, and turn out the way we dream they will." (Marilyn Heins, M.D., *New York Times Magazine*, 7 March 1999, p. 14.)

Can corporal punishment injure self-esteem?

Yes. Parents who are reduced to physical discipline for correction demonstrate to themselves and the child that, despite being older and more experienced, they are not smart enough to assert influence and get their point across in any other way. "Might is right," is the message the child receives, and dreams of the day when he or she has grown too big to be pushed around by parents anymore. "I'm teaching the child respect for authority," contends the parent, when in fact what the child is learning is *contempt:* "Just 'cause they're bigger, they think they can bully and hit me any way they like!"

It is worth remembering what the American Academy of Pediatrics has to say on the subject of physical punishment: "Spanking may relieve a parent's frustration for the moment and extinguish the undesirable behavior for a brief time. But it is the least effective way to discipline. It is harmful emotionally to both parent and child. Not only can it result in physical harm, but it teaches the child that violence is an acceptable way to discipline or express anger. While stopping the behavior temporarily, it does not teach alternative behavior. It also interferes with the development of trust, a sense of security, and effective communication. (Spanking often becomes the method of communication.) It also may cause emotional pain and resentment...Physical punishment is rarely if ever effective. Rather, it usually occurs when a parent is unable to manage his or her own anger or frustration effectively and thus inappropriately resorts to aggression. When a child's aggressive behavior is met with more aggressive behavior from a parent, things usually get worse, not better." (See Suggested Reading, Schor, 1995, pp. 196, 207.)

Are there any signs of low self-esteem that parents might be on the alert for in their children?

Yes, but they are only possibilities not certainties, suggestive but not conclusive. A few signs that a boy or girl might be experiencing low self-esteem could be:

- If the child aspiring to being perfect becomes angry or despondent when making normal mistakes
- If the child is out to prove that "nothing is wrong" with him or her
- If the child makes comparisons about being superior or inferior to other people
- If the child automatically apologizes when anything goes wrong, whether or not he or she had anything to do with it
- If the child has to have the last word or final say in an argument
- If the child feels unable to truthfully admit or sincerely apologize when he or she has done something wrong
- If the child feels compelled to make excuses when not doing as well as he or she would like
- If the child would rather put himself or herself down than honestly acknowledge doing something well
- If the child's feeling good about himself or herself depends on always keeping other people pleased
- If the child gives up when a first effort fails instead of trying again
- If a child blames others for what he or she did wrong

- If the child tries to take credit for what others have done well
- If the child cheats, or lies, or steals to get his or her needs met
- If the child refuses to accept compliments from other people or refuses to give compliments to other people
- If a child's personal worth depends on having the very best or most expensive possessions
- If the child needs to put other people's efforts or achievements down.
- If the child can spend money on other people but not on himself or herself
- If the child refuses to say what he or she is thinking for fear of getting into a disagreement
- If the child always needs to get his or her way to feel okay
- If the child needs alcohol or drugs to be socially confident, to cope with challenges, or to escape from painful feelings
- If the child continues to accept treatment from others he or she admits is hurtful and unhealthy
- If the child refuses to try something new for fear of failure
- If the child can't refuse friends urging him or her to go along with group misbehavior
- If the child acts self-destructively in any way

Is there such a thing as having too much self-esteem?

Yes. People who prize themselves too highly often believe they are superior, are always right, are entitled to special consideration and treatment, need tolerate no disagreement, know it all (or at least all that is worth knowing), deserve to be given their way, and should be allowed to rule over the lives of others. Many tyrants, petty and great, from the spoiled child to the cruel despot, have had extremely high self-esteem, *at other people's expense*. The best antidotes to excessive self-esteem are *humility* ("I am no more or less special than anybody else") and *mutuality* ("I believe in two-way relationships, where the needs of each party are equally valued and both served").

If there was one simple prescription for preserving strong self-esteem, what whould it be?

"There's a lot of talk about self-esteem these days...It seems pretty basic to me. If you want to feel proud of yourself, you've got to do things you can feel proud of. Feelings follow actions." This statement was made by Oseola McCarty, a washerwoman who gave her life savings of $150,000 to fund scholarships at the University of Southern Mississippi. (*New York Times*, 28 September 1999, p. C31.)

GLOSSARY

Abandonment the painful experience of being deserted by a loved one.

Abuse behavior by a parent that emotionally, verbally, physically, or sexually inflicts injury to the well-being and safety of a child.

ADD (Attention Deficit Disorder) a condition characterized by such features as short attention span, impulsiveness, distractibility, and restless energy that the child has difficulty being able to control.

Addiction coming to compulsively depend on a self-destructive substance or activity for survival.

Adolescence that period of growth between when the boy or girl begins the separation from childhood (around ages ten to twelve) and when he or she becomes grown up enough to claim young adult independence eight to ten years later.

Depression a severe state of despondency in which a person becomes emotionally stuck, typically feeling trapped, hopeless, helpless, angry, and worthless, with very little available energy or motivation to make any positive change.

Early adolescent achievement drop less adequate academic performance resulting from a young person, typically in late elementary or early middle school, becoming so distracted and disaffected by adolescent growth that energy previously invested in accomplishing schoolwork now becomes channeled into resisting it.

Expectation a mental set that people use to create a frame of reference for the present and to anticipate the reality to come.

Expressive inhibition the process of shutting down one's creative expression for fear of, or from the experience of, being made to feel self-conscious or look foolish in the eyes of others.

Next-step reluctance in late adolescence (around ages sixteen to eighteen), when the older teenager purposely delays preparations for moving on to more independence from fear of not being ready for the next level of responsibility.

Punitive coaching tactics of humiliation, intimidation, and dissatisfaction that many coaches, particularly of secondary school-age children, use to control and motivate players.

Retention the decision to hold a student back a grade for reason of academic insufficiency or social immaturity.

Stimulus Overload Adjustment (SOA) a possible culturally conditioned response that children may have to growing up in a technologically overstimulating world, developing a set of behaviors similar to those often used to describe ADD.

SUGGESTED READING

Briggs, Dorothy Corkille. *Your Child's Self-Esteem.* New York: Doubleday, 1970.

Fassler, David G., M.D., and Lynne S. Dumas. *Help Me, I'm Sad.* New York: Viking Penguin, 1997.

Flach, Frederic, M.D. *The Secret Strength of Depression.* New York: Bantam, 1975.

McNamara, Barry and Francine. *Keys to Parenting a Child with Attention Deficit Disorder.* Hauppauge, New York: Barron's Educational Series, Inc., 1993.

Merck Research Laboratories. *The Merck Manual of Medical Information.* West Point, Pennsylvania: The Merck Manuals Department, 1997.

Pickhardt, Carl E. *Keys to Parenting the Only Child.* Hauppauge, New York: Barron's Educational Series, Inc., 1997.

———. *Keys to Raising a Drug-free Child.* Hauppauge, New York: Barron's Educational Series, Inc., 1999.

———. *Keys to Single Parenting.* Hauppauge, New York: Barron's Educational Series, Inc., 1996.

———. *Keys to Successful Stepfathering.* Hauppauge, New York: Barron's Educational Series, Inc., 1997.

———. *Parenting the Teenager.* P.O. Box 50022, Austin, Texas 78763, 1983.

———. *The Case of the Scary Divorce.* Washington D.C.: Magination Press, The American Psychological Association, 1997.

Pipher, Mary, Ph.D. *Reviving Ophelia—Saving the Selves of Adolescent Girls*. New York: Ballantine, 1994.

Pollack, William. *Real Boys*. New York: Random House, 1998.

Schaefer, Charles E., Ph.D. and Howard L. Millman, Ph.D. *How to Help Children with Common Problems*. New York: Penguin, 1981.

Schor, Edward L., M.D. *Caring for Your School-Age Child*. New York: Bantam, 1995.

Seligman, Martin E. P., Ph.D. *The Optimistic Child*. New York: HarperCollins, 1995.

Steinberg, Laurence, Ph.D. and Ann Levine. *You & Your Adolescent*. New York: Harper & Row, 1990.

INDEX